BATTERED WOMEN, SHATTERED LIVES

by

Kathleen H. Hofeller, Ph.D.

Published by

R & E RESEARCH ASSOCIATES, INCORPORATED
Publishers
936 Industrial Avenue
Palo Alto, California 94303

Library of Congress Card Catalog Number
82-50377

I.S.B.N.
0-88247-687-4

TO: My husband and daughter for their love and support

TABLE OF CONTENTS

INTRODUCTION

By the time you have finished reading this introduction, the chances are that a woman will have been beaten. It may be the wife of an executive who can no longer cope with the pressures of his job. It may be a woman whose husband comes home drunk—again. It could be your neighbor, a friend, your sister, or your own mother. Maybe you yourself are living with a violent man.

Whatever your personal experiences, the fact that you are reading this book means you are concerned about the problem of wife abuse, and for that, I thank you. The efforts of people like you will be needed if we are ever to eliminate the violence that occurs in millions of American homes. And it is important for us to think about homes and *families*, because when a woman is battered, it is not only she who suffers. Domestic violence can shatter the lives of all concerned—the woman, her husband, their children, their relatives. Even those who, like myself, have had only indirect contact with wife abuse, find that their lives are changed; it is impossible to work in this field and not be personally touched by your experiences.

In compiling the material for this book, I have drawn from several different sources: the published works of other researchers; my informal discussions with psychologists, social workers, paraprofessionals and peer counselors, doctors, nurses, and individuals in the criminal justice system; my own experiences in helping establish House of Ruth, a shelter for battered women in Southern California; results

vii

from my doctoral study involving in-depth interviews with battered women; and two years as a phone counselor on a domestic violence hot-line.

Over the past few years, I have come in contact with a great number of battered women, and quite honestly, many times I have been greatly distressed by what I encountered: the pain, apprehension and utter despair in the voices of women who called the hot-line for help; the distraught faces of friends and relatives who, unable to successfully intervene, could only stand by helplessly as someone they loved was emotionally and physically battered; the fear and confusion in the eyes of the children, truly the "forgotten victims" of wife abuse.

At one point, I thought that being constantly confronted with such problems would eventually make me discouraged and cynical about human nature. Instead, however, my interviews with formerly battered wives frequently left me feeling optimistic. For the experience of having successfully dealt with a violent man had given many women a new-found sense of competence, independence, and self-worth. These women liked themselves, and it showed—in their warmth and openness toward me, and in their desire to do whatever they could to help other battered women. I was impressed by their courage, determination, and resiliency. In short, women can and do manage to get out of violent relationships.

Of course, wife abuse is not just a "women's issue"—it is a *social* issue, and in order to reduce the level of family violence, all of us need to be aware of the ways in which we can help. Therefore, one of the primary purposes in writing this book was to provide practical, "down-to-earth" advice on dealing with domestic violence. If you are interested in developing community programs, there is information to help you get started. If you know someone who is being abused, I hope I can give you a better idea of what she is going through. If you yourself are living with violence, I hope you will feel encouraged to begin the process of regaining a sense of your own strength, vitality, and purpose.

CHAPTER I

MYTH AND REALITY

The case histories presented in this book are drawn from actual interviews with battered women. Names and details have been changed to protect the anonymity of all concerned.

Andrea

Physically and sexually abused by her father, Andrea's childhood had been a nightmare. Then she met Roger, the first person who had ever shown her any real affection. When he proposed, Andrea was sure she had finally found happiness.

Corrie

Corrie was one of eight children, the daughter of a sharecropper. She became pregnant at fifteen and neither she nor her family could provide for the baby. Corrie felt she had no choice but to marry Joe, the father of her child.

Janet

Raised by strict, over-protective parents, Janet longed for freedom and the opportunity to be out on her own. David was handsome, charming, and opened new vistas for Janet. When he asked her to marry him, it was like a dream come true.

Andrea, Corrie, Janet — Three different women, from three different backgrounds. Yet all entered marriage with the same hope of building a happy, fulfilling life. This hope, however, was not to be realized. Instead, these women would endure the fear, pain, and despair of being battered and brutalized by the very men who professed to love them.

There are literally millions of women like Andrea, Corrie, and Janet. It is estimated that at least 1.8 million American women are battered by their husbands or boyfriends.[1] Obviously, wife abuse is very prevalent in our society. However, only recently have social scientists begun to study the problem. Although public awareness of domestic violence has certainly increased over the past few years, many myths and stereotypes still exist. The following are some commonly made statements about wife abuse. Do you know which are true, and which are false?

- Wife abuse only occurs in lower socio-economic groups.

- Battered women must enjoy the abuse. Otherwise, they would take the children and leave.

- If a women gets beaten, it's probably because she provoked her husband.

- The battered woman who is serious about solving the problem could have her husband arrested and put in jail.

- Most abused women grew up in families where there was violence.

2

- If a battered woman remarries, she usually chooses another violent man.

Each of these statements is false—a common misconception about wife abuse. What is it *really* like to live with violence? Let Andrea, Corrie, and Janet tell you their own stories.

Andrea

Andrea was one of the most nervous and tense women I spoke with. Her first words after "Hello," were "Is it okay if I smoke?", and when I said "Sure," she was noticeably relieved. She chained smoked throughout the interview, and when her fingers weren't busy with a cigarette, she played nervously with her clothes or gripped the arm of her chair.

Andrea was dressed in a long sleeved plaid cotton blouse, a wrap-around denim skirt, and sandals. She had a slender build and a fair complexion. Her long, blonde hair was worn in a single, waist length braid, and she could have been a very pretty woman. But Andrea's life had taken its toll, and now I sat across from a woman whose features were hardened and whose expression reflected anger and defiance. Clearly embittered by the cruelty and injustice she had suffered, the only time she softened was when she talked about her daughter.

When I asked her to describe her childhood, Andrea took a long puff on her cigarette, stiffened up in her chair as if preparing for battle, and began. "My childhood was about the closest thing to hell that I can imagine. My father was really two people. When he went off to work or was out for a social event he was Mr. _____, the successful businessman, prominent citizen, and a pillar of the church. But when he came home he was my father, cruel and frightening. You see, he was a very heavy drinker, and when he got drunk, which was quite frequently, he got violent. Most of the time it was the furniture

3

or the dishes or my mother who got the worst of it, but sometimes he'd take out after me and my younger sisters, too. My father was a very strict disciplinarian, and any of the three of us could be beaten severely for the slightest infraction. The first incident that I remember clearly was when I was about five or six years old. I had done something wrong—so help me I can't remember what it was—anyway, my father decided that he would teach me a lesson. He took his belt and beat the living daylights out of me. I had so many bruises that my mother had me stay home from school for the next couple of days. After all, we had an image to maintain and we couldn't have little Andrea 'blowing our cover.'

It was bad enough that he'd beat me, but what I really hated was when he'd go after my little sisters. I felt very protective. After all, when you're only three or four, you're pretty defenseless. God, I can remember screaming at my father and trying to pull him off of them and saying that it was my fault so he would turn on me instead. Throughout all of this my mother never intervened once. So help me, there are times when I think I'll never forgive her for that. But, I guess she was just as scared of him as we were. She probably figured that if she tried to stop him, he'd just beat the hell out of her, too.

By the time I was eight or nine, I can remember being in a hurry to grow up so I could leave home. Of course, if I had known what was going to happen to me as I became a woman, I would not have been so eager. The first time I realized I was 'in for it' was when I was about eleven and had begun to develop. I was sitting, reading, in the livingroom, and my father was drunk as was so often his custom after dinner. He motioned to me to come over and sit on his lap. Now, my father had never shown any of us attention like that. So, I was surprised and pleased. I went over and sat on his lap. Well, it wasn't too long before I figured out what he *really* had in mind, and it was not fatherly affection. When he started fondling me in very private places, I was horrified. I jumped off his lap and ran to my bedroom.

4

After that I avoided being alone with him as much as possible, but one night he finally caught up with me. He came into my room, drunk, of course, and climbed into bed with me. He said, 'I'm going to show you what it's like to be with a man. That's what fathers do for their daughters. But it's just our secret, understand?' Well, he kissed me all over and fondled me and everything, but he didn't really rape me. He rubbed himself between my thighs and came that way. When he left he said, 'If you ever tell anybody I was here, I'll beat you to death.'

Well, this went on for several more months until I just couldn't stand it any more. I felt so dirty and guilty, I had to do something. I thought about telling my mother, but I figured it wouldn't do any good. I mean she had never done anything in the past to help us. Finally, in desperation, I decided I'd talk to the minister in charge of the youth group at our church. It took me a week to get up enough courage, but I did it. Boy, was that ever a mistake. He called in my mother and father to talk about it, and my parents were livid. They denied it, of course, and when I got home they were furious. I can still remember the scene. My father would slap me across the face and demand to know why I had lied. When I said I wasn't lying, he'd hit me again. My mother screamed at me, too, for humiliating them. Finally I began to hurt so much, I had to make him stop. So I said yes, I had lied, I was sorry, and I would never do it again. That seemed to satisfy him and I was sent up to my room. The bruises didn't go away for days, but I'll tell you, he didn't come bothering me anymore, so it was worth all the pain. After that, I vowed I would get out of that house as soon as I could. It was a hard decision, though, because I knew my little sisters would be without anyone to protect them. But, I figured I would never survive if I stayed. And, when I was fifteen, I did run away. I went to a friend's house for awhile, but the police caught up with me and brought me home. I was disappointed, but I vowed I would try again, and the day after I graduated from high school I left for good. I shared an apartment with a friend on the other side of town and got a job as a waitress. The customers seemed to like me and I did real well.

Now, this girl I was living with, Margie, was nineteen and very wise in the ways of the world. I don't suppose she was a very good influence in any department, but the absolutely worst thing she ever did was to introduce me to Roger. Margie worked at the same restaurant that I did and she had met Roger there. He told her that he wanted to talk to me, but I really didn't want anything to do with *any* man. Well, he persisted and she persisted, so finally, just to get them both off my back, I had a cup of coffee with him. He seemed nice enough and was the perfect gentleman. What an act he put on for me! At any rate, he kept calling and calling and wanting another coffee date. Finally, I gave in. I wasn't that eager to date, but Margie kept after me. She'd say, 'Come on Andrea, go out on a real date with him. You need some fun in life.' So finally I did. I guess we went to a movie or something like that. When we got home we started to neck. Just kissing was okay, but when his hands started moving to those places, all I could think of was my father, and I absolutely 'froze.' He asked me what was wrong. So, in kind of sugar-coated terms, I told him what had happened to me. He seemed really sympathetic and didn't press me any further—at least not right then.

We started dating steadily after that, and I managed to stay a virgin for about six months. Some record. Anyway, one time when I had been drinking quite a bit, he finally got me in bed with him. It was not all that spectacular, I assure you, but it didn't kill me either, and that in itself was a pleasant surprise. What wasn't so pleasant was my guilt afterwards. I felt terrible. You see, part of my parents' strange moral code was that you didn't sleep with a man unless you intended to marry him, and I was in no way ready to settle down. I mean, at that time I wasn't sure that I *ever* wanted to get married. But Margie kept pressuring me. 'Go ahead. You ought to marry him. He's a nice guy.' Frankly, I think I was beginning to cramp her style a bit. She wanted to branch out, and there was old Andrea in the next bedroom. Besides, Roger seemed to really care about me, and no one had ever done that before. So, when he asked me to marry him, I said 'yes.' Believe me, never again will I say 'yes' so quickly to any man.

You see, once we were married I began to find out that Roger had these 'little' problems. Like, he had a temper and when he was angry he'd throw things—dishes, ashtrays, anything that was handy. Sometimes he'd even smash his fist into the wall. Seems to me we did an awful lot of patching and plastering in those days. He didn't hit me until about three years after we had been married. His mother had died and he became very depressed. Now, I thought this was kind of strange, because he'd always disliked his mother. In fact, whenever he talked about her you could almost see the hatred in those beady, black eyes of his. And you know, I can't say as I really blame him. His parents were divorced when Roger was eight, and his mom remarried when he was ten. She and her new husband kept Roger's two younger brothers with them, but sent him off to military school. I don't think he ever forgave her for that.

At any rate, we were sitting on the couch together, talking about something, when all of a sudden without any warning he lunges at me, grabs me around the neck and starts choking me. He shook me and said, 'Don't you ever look at me that way again! Apologize, you bitch!' I was absolutely terrified. I tried to say 'I'm sorry, I'm sorry,' but I didn't have much breath. I finally managed to get some kind of apology out, and that seemed to satisfy him. He threw me down on the couch and stormed out. I figured well, he's really upset because of his mother. After all, no matter how much he hated her she was still his mother. So I kind of let it go at that. I tried to concentrate on his better qualities and just go on with it.

Well, the longer we were married, the harder it was to find any of those better qualities. For one thing, although he was very successful, we never seemed to have enough money. You see, Roger wanted to

7

spend it all on himself. Like he'd go out and charge up $2000 worth of clothes for himself in a single afternoon! And hobbies! Oh, did he have hobbies! Fishing, hunting, gun collecting, scuba diving—you name it. He'd buy all this expensive equipment, and then he'd get tired of it and it would sit in the garage and gather dust. But would he let me sell any of it? Oh no, absolutely not. So sometimes we had trouble paying our bills even though I was working almost the whole time we were married.

Roger was also a very jealous person. Strangely, it didn't come out until after Sandra was born. So help me, Sandra is the only good thing that has ever happened to me. She was such a good baby. Even Roger seemed to love her. He showed her off to everyone and was very proud of her. And when she was little he'd help take care of her, which really surprised me. Oh, he'd never change diapers, but he'd feed her and talk to her. But then when she started taking on her own looks and personality—I guess she was about five months old—he started saying things like, 'That's not my baby—she doesn't look a thing like me. Who's the *real* father?' Well, that was absolutely absurd and he knew it. I had never slept with anyone but him. Well, this jealousy just got worse and worse. I mean, he'd drive me to work, wait in the car until I went in, and then pick me up on the dot of noon to bring me home. We even had to stop taking the paper because he thought I was having an affair with the paper boy. And, whenever I went out on my own I had to give him a list of everything I was going to do in the afternoon and how long it would take. If he called me and I wasn't back, he'd be furious when he got home. He might not always beat me for it, but you knew something in the house would get broken. Towards the very end, I found that he'd even put a tap on our phone. Can you imagine that?

At the beginning of our marriage, Roger seemed to blow up on kind of a regular basis, maybe once every three months or so. I got so that I could see it building up inside of him and then something, any-

8

thing, could set it off. Roger always claimed that he didn't know what he was doing when he'd fly into these rages, but I think he did. Like, he was always careful to aim his blows so they wouldn't show much. He'd hit me in the stomach or on my shoulders and arms. I wore a lot of long sleeved, turtleneck blouses back then. He would avoid my face because that was really obvious, and dear Roger was very image conscious. On top of that, he could be right in the middle of beating me, kicking me, or throwing things at me, and if there was a knock at the door or the phone rang, he could just stop cold. I mean, he'd go and answer the door as if nothing was wrong. I remember one time in particular. It was horrible. We'd been arguing, and I just knew that I was going to really get beaten up. Well, right in the middle of all this, some friends dropped in for visit. Somehow I managed to get Joanne off in the other room and said, 'Listen, you've got to take me with you. You've got to let me go with you. I just know Roger is going to really hurt me. Something terrible is going to happen and I've got to get out of her. I'll grab Sandy and we'll go.' I was so desperate, I was begging and pleading. Well, I just couldn't believe Joanne. She said, 'Oh, now Andrea, you're exaggerating. Roger isn't like that; he'd never hit you. Besides it would ruin our friendship if we interfered. It isn't really our problem, you know.' Well, so much for that friend. And so much for me after they left, 'cause Roger took up where he left off, and I ended up getting a beating. I was really mad at my so-called friends, but you see, Roger could be very nice to other people. He was friendly and could be very charming—even kind. He was actually good to me at times, although those times got fewer and farther between the longer we were married.

Roger also began to get after me about sex. He was always complaining that I was frigid, and that sleeping with me was like screwing a cold fish. Well, it was partly his own fault. Sure, I'd had a bad childhood, but Roger made things worse. He'd come in and say, 'I want to try something new.' So he'd keep doing it, and finally I'd say, 'I don't really like that so much.' But he'd keep doing it and doing it, and finally I'd say, 'Hey, I really like that after all. Let's do it some more.' Then he'd stop and I'd never hear about it again. So I got smart. It took me awhile, but I got smart. And I liked *everything*. I became the most liberated woman in bed you have ever seen. Well, I guess Roger tired of that game after awhile and he went back to complaining that I just wasn't good, and that I never wanted sex. He never actually forced me or anything, but it was a problem. Hell, *everything* eventually became a problem for us.

Roger wanted to control every aspect of my life. He wouldn't let me go out and he wouldn't let me see any of my friends from work. If Roger and I went out together, it was always with his friends, and we always went where *he* wanted to go. So, I really didn't have anyone to talk to. I certainly wasn't going to go to my parents, not after what I'd been through with them. In fact, I never told anyone about the beatings until the very last. I was so embarrassed, I was sure that everyone would think it was all my fault, because I was such a horrible person. I mean, my parents had told me that, Roger told me that, and I believed it, too. It sounds crazy now, but back then I blamed myself for what was happening to me. I told myself that if I would only try harder to be better—a better wife, mother, person—that the beatings would stop. And when the beatings didn't stop, I just figured I hadn't done well enough yet.

Well, it wasn't too long before I got to feeling really depressed. And, I started drinking. Never until after work, though, because my job was too important to me to risk getting fired. Sandra was in day care in the morning and in the afternoon she just sort of fended for herself. I still feel really bad about that time in my life, you know, because I neglected her so much. The worst thing that ever happened was when she was about four years old. I had been heating up some soup on the stove for her lunch and I forgot about it. Well, she was wandering around and she went into the kitchen and grabbed at the handle and it spilled over her. She started screaming like crazy, and that sobered me up fast. I rushed her to the hospital and the doctor was looking at me like he didn't believe me. I think he thought I'd spilled it on her on purpose. But I hadn't. I love my little girl. Anyway, I was awfully lucky because it wasn't too bad. They bandaged her up and I took her home. Of course, Roger was furious. I was obviously a terrible mother and that gave him a reason to beat me up again. I'm sorry to say that that incident didn't slow my drinking down any. I guess I was lucky that there weren't any more accidents. I really didn't want to hurt Sandra. I'll tell you, though, one time I came very close. Roger was being particularly impossible and there was Sandra, sitting in the corner crying for no good reason at all. I grabbed her by the shoulders and shook her really hard. She had this horrified look on her face and all of a sudden I saw what I was doing. It scared me. I didn't want to be like my father. But you know, I think it was a good thing that that happened, because it upset me so much that I got up the nerve to call the child abuse hotline. The woman who answered was very understanding and she helped me a lot. From that time on I really watched myself every minute I was with Sandra. When I was on the verge of getting angry with her, I'd try to control myself as best I could and just hold everything in.

Things went about the same for around six months. Then Roger got a promotion. That should have meant that things would be better for us, but because of his new position and higher salary he decided that I should stop working. Well, work was just about the only thing that was keeping me from going insane. It was a place where I knew I was doing a good job and where people liked me. But Roger said that he was an executive now and that it would look bad for his wife to be working. People would think he couldn't provide for his family. Besides, he had decided that I ought to be home more. He wanted to be able to come home for lunch at 11:30 and I was supposed to have it ready for him when he got there. Now, that would have been impossible because I didn't finish until 12:30. Needless to say, we got into quite an argument about whether or not I should work. Our argument turned into a shouting match which continued even at the dinner table. When I served him his meal, he looked down at it and said, 'This is slop. It isn't fit for pigs. You can't even cook for me because you're either too drunk or you're thinking about your Goddamn job and your lousy lovers.' He took his plate and threw it against the wall. It was spaghetti that night, wouldn't you know, so I had nice red tomato sauce all over the kitchen. Now, up until that moment, I had never tried to fight back. But I just couldn't take it anymore. Making me quit work was just the last straw. So, out of frustration more than anything else, I picked up my plate and threw it back at him. It only grazed his head. I wish it had hit him, but it didn't. Well, that got him really mad. He stood up and knocked the table over. Naturally, that scared Sandra, so she started crying. Roger yelled at her to go to her room, but she just stood there, screaming, 'Don't hurt Mommy, don't hurt Mommy.' Finally he grabbed her by the arm, dragged her to her room, and slammed the door. I knew immediately that I had gone too far. So I said, 'Okay, okay, I'm not going to work. I'll quit; I'll do whatever you want.' Obviously that wasn't enough, because he started into his routine. It was always the same. First he'd start calling me names and screaming at me, then he'd break something or put his fist into the wall or kick a door. He'd work himself up into a rage, and then if I couldn't run out of the house in time, he'd come after me.

Anyway, like I said, I was really scared this time, so I started screaming. I was yelling, 'Don't kill me! Help!' or something like that and I started throwing things at him, too. We made an awful lot of noise, which turned out to be a good thing, because he grabbed me around the neck and started choking me. This wasn't the first time he'd ever choked me, but he was so violent that time. I'll never forget how horrible it felt to have his fingers tightening around my throat. I was starting to black out when I heard a pounding at the door. It was one of

12

our neighbors. Roger pushed me into the bedroom and I fell onto the floor. I could just barely make out his words when he answered the door. Roger was calm and composed, and I think he said something like that I had accidentally fallen. I don't think our neighbor really believed that, but he didn't want to get involved. Nobody ever wants to get involved. So he left. At any rate, that interruption seemed to bring Roger to his senses. I heard the front door slam again, and Roger didn't come back for hours. You know something funny, when I had almost blacked out, I thought, 'This is it, this is the end. Lord, take me, I'm going to die.' And I really wasn't all that upset about it. I've never told anybody else before, but when I was married to Roger I thought a lot about committing suicide. That had always seemed to me a very cowardly thing to do, but there were times when I figured that was the only way out. You know, sometimes you hurt so much, it seems as though nothing in the world could ever take away the pain. The only thing that kept me from killing myself was Sandra. There was no way that I could leave her alone with Roger.

Believe it or not, even after that incident I was still trying to think of some way to keep working. But it turned out that I didn't really have any choice at all because I started getting these pains in my stomach. I tried to ignore it, but it got so bad I just knew I had to do something about it, so I finally went to the doctor. You know what I had? Bleeding ulcers. The doctor wanted me to go into the hospital but I said I couldn't. He said it was either that or I could go home and get worse and maybe even bleed to death. So they admitted me into the hospital. Now, while I was in there it was Roger's birthday, right? And he always liked to make a big thing out of it. Well, I was still pretty sick, and all he could do was telephone me and say, 'Why didn't you call me and wish me a happy birthday? Couldn't you even send a card? You were supposed to give me a party.' And do you know, I actually apologized to him. You'd never catch me doing that for any man today, but I did then. I apologized.

13

I stayed in the hospital for about three days. When I first got home, Roger was really nice to me. I thought, 'Wow, things are really going to change. Maybe we can make it after all.' But it didn't take too long for us both to get back into our old ways. Of course, I did have to stop drinking because of the ulcers. I wanted to go to AA, but Roger said, 'No wife of mine is going to be seen at AA. I won't be disgraced.' And I said, 'Look, they use first names. They won't know who I am.' But he wouldn't allow it. Well, deep down I knew that if I kept on drinking, it would end up killing me. I don't know, maybe some old survival instinct in me surfaced. But anyway, I decided to take a chance. I had one close friend from work and I told her what was happening and what I had to do. She was just terrific. She stayed at the house with Sandra while I went to an AA meeting and she would feed Roger some line if he happened to call while I was out. It really helped going, you know, because I met people there who cared about me. And a lot of times I would just end up talking to someone on the phone when I couldn't get to a meeting.

We went on like this for about three months. Roger hadn't been violent, and I really thought maybe it would be okay. I wasn't all that happy, but I figured this was the best I was ever going to get. Well, I should have known better, because it didn't last. The whole thing exploded again one night when Roger came in drunk. He wasn't much of a drinker, but he had been at some party and he was really obnoxious. He came in around one in the morning, shook me awake, and for some crazy reason demanded to have Sandra wake up and greet her father. I said, 'Listen, Roger, she's in bed. She's asleep. Leave her alone.' Well, that just made him mad, and he went stomping off toward Sandra's bedroom. I followed after him 'cause I had no idea what he might do. Well, he stormed into her room, and yanked her out of bed. Of course she started crying—you can't do that to a child—and then it made him mad that she cried, so he started slapping her in the face. Naturally I came to her defense and tried to pull him off her. I

14

grabbed his arms, and as I did he swung around and hit me in the stomach with his fist. I felt this hideous flash of pain go right through me, and I doubled up, falling back against the wall. He pushed by me, saying, 'I'm going to teach you a lesson, bitch.' I didn't know what to do. I was in too much pain to grab Sandra and run for it, but I had no idea what Roger was going to do. It wasn't long before I found out, 'cause just as I was managing to straighten up, back came Roger with one of his guns. He pushed Sandra back into her room, slammed the door, and ordered her not to come out. Then he grabbed me by the arm and pushed me down on the couch. Before I knew it, I felt the gun at the back of my head. Roger was standing behind the couch. Then I heard this horrible voice. Roger said something like, 'Okay, you whore, now you're going to tell me who you've been fucking. Tell me who your lovers are or I'll pull the trigger.' I denied it, of course, but that just made him angrier. Finally, I decided I'd better play along, so I lied and said I'd been sleeping with one of the men at the office. So he said, 'Okay, this is for you,' and he pulled the trigger. I heard that 'click,' and nearly fainted. The gun wasn't loaded, but it nearly scared me to death anyway. Well, Roger thought that was really funny. I heard him laughing all the way to our bedroom. I was too stunned to move. I just couldn't believe what was happening to me. Slowly, very slowly, it dawned on me that if I stayed with Roger, he might really kill me some day. So, that night I decided, 'No more; I've got to get out.' Now, I had threatened to leave before and Roger had said he'd find me and kill me. He said he'd hire a private detective if he had to. But this time I knew that it was going to be me or him, and I had determined that I was going to make it. I also had to think about my daughter and her future.

It was all quiet in our bedroom, so I tiptoed in. Roger had passed out, thank God. So I went through the house and packed up everything I thought we might need. Then I rummaged through Roger's trousers and took every bit of money in them (that sure felt good). I put Sandra in the car and I drove and drove and drove. Sandra fell asleep almost immediately. I think she knew she could finally relax. We ended up staying in a motel that night about a hundred miles out of town. I really don't know what possessed me to drive so far. I guess it was just that every minute I drove I knew I was getting farther and farther away from Roger. And the farther away I got, the better I felt. It was as if I could drive to the other side of the earth and there still wouldn't be enough distance between us.

I remember that night in the motel was really eye opening. Roger didn't find us and I think it was probably the first time that I saw that he was not all-powerful. That was a very important thing for me to find out. Of course, I didn't sleep much that night; I kept hearing things and wondering when he would appear pounding at the door. The next morning, Sandra and I were both alive and well and I certainly never expected that to happen. But in the morning I had to make some really hard decisions. I knew I'd have to go back if only to get the rest of our things and to file for divorce and so forth. So we had breakfast and started back. On the way home I planned out exactly what I would do. First, I drove by our house. Luckily, his car was gone. So I got all the things I thought we'd need and put them in the car. Next, I went to the bank, thinking I'd cash a check. Well, that creep had already been there and had taken everything out of the account. At that point I was beginning to get kind of panicky. I couldn't think of anyplace I could go and really feel safe. I didn't want to involve my close friends, and besides, I knew Roger would come looking for us there. I was about ready to give up when I remembered that hotline I had used when I had lost control with Sandra. The counselor gave me the number of a crisis line for battered women and I called that. Well, to make a long story short, the shelters were full and there wasn't going to be a place for us for at least two or three days—they just didn't have room. I had about fifty dollars left, so Sandra and I stayed in this cheap motel for two nights, and we lived on McDonald's hamburgers. I also went down and applied for welfare, but I couldn't get any money for a week, and I honestly don't know what I would have done if we hadn't gotten into the shelter. We could only stay there for a week, but it really helped me. Sandra began to relax. She had to sleep on a mattress on the floor, but it was better than being alone in that motel and certainly better than going back to Roger. The best part was that I got a chance to talk to other women whose husbands had beaten them. That was very important to me, because until then I'd thought my mother and I were just about the only ones in the world that this had ever happened to.

A counselor also helped me get a restraining order and I filed for divorce. That took about a week. Then I went back home and did everything they told me to do. I changed the locks, left the lights on at night, and so forth. But Roger kept coming around and bothering us. I thought about learning to use one of his guns but I just didn't want to do that. Well, one night he nearly broke down the door. I called the police and explained to them that we were separated but it didn't seem to do a lot of good. I wanted them to arrest him but they wouldn't do it. I changed my phone number several times but Roger always got the new one somehow. I moved three times in the space of one year, but all he had to do to find us was to follow me home from work. After about a year of that I decided that I just couldn't live that way anymore. Even though he wasn't beating me up or even living with me, I always was afraid that he might come and hurt us. I mean, he still had control over me. I had thought that I was getting away from all that by divorcing him. Finally, I just packed up and we moved to California, halfway across the country. I've changed my name, and I suppose I should let him know where I am but I haven't and I don't intend to.

All in all, I feel pretty safe now. But if I see a man that even looks like Roger, my stomach knots up. Because Roger is out there somewhere. I don't know, maybe in my mind he'll be following me forever. At any rate, I've begun dating a man and he keeps wanting me to move in with him. I might, but I'm going to be really careful this time. Frankly, I still don't trust men very much. I don't know if I ever will. I mean, first it was my father and then Roger. It seems like what every man wants is to get you in bed. I think a lot about Sandra. She's seven years old now and I know all the pain she'll probably go through because of men. It makes me think of a book that I read in high school once—Dickens' *Great Expectations*, I guess it was. There was this old lady who kept a little girl in her house and then had a boy come to visit every week. Well, she taught that girl how to use men instead of having them use her. She taught her not to trust them so she wouldn't be hurt. The old lady was pretty smart, and if I had a choice, that's what I'd want for Sandra—great expectations."

MYTHS

1. **WIFE ABUSE ONLY OCCURS IN LOWER SOCIO-ECONOMIC GROUPS.**

    Domestic violence is a problem that cuts across all economic lines and knows no boundary of race, religion, occupation, or age. However, lower economic groups are often over-represented in statistics on wifebeating. This occurs because the middle or upper class woman simply has more resources. She can consult a private physician or psychiatrist rather than go to a public hospital or social service agency. She also may be more reluctant to call the police because of the effect it might have on her husband's job and reputation.

18

2. BATTERED WOMEN MUST ENJOY THE ABUSE. OTHERWISE THEY WOULD TAKE THE CHILDREN AND LEAVE.

This statement reflects the widespread belief that battered women are masochistic and like to be beaten. However, this is simply not the case. I do not know of any woman who found it sexually arousing to have her eyes blackened or her nose broken. Wife abuse bears no resemblance to playful wrestling or "love pats." The "pats" a battered woman receives are likely to leave her bruised, bleeding—or in the hospital. If these women do not derive pleasure from the abuse, then why *do* they stay? There are a number of reasons.

To begin with, many women remain in violent situations because they feel sorry for their husbands. At first glance, it may seem incomprehensible that a woman could feel sympathy for the man who causes her so much pain. However, it must be remembered that our society still expects women to be nurturant, loving, and forgiving. Since men are sometimes contrite and beg for forgiveness after a beating, a woman may view divorce as the abandonment of a person who desperately needs help. To do that would mean she had failed in her role as a devoted, patient, and compassionate wife.

Women also find it difficult to get out of a violent situation because of the psychological effects of living with a wife-beater. Almost without exception, battered women are subjected to varying degrees of emotional abuse. Wives are told that they are worthless, incompetent, stupid, and incapable of surviving without masculine help and direction. Women are criticized for the way they wear their hair, the way they keep house, and the way they raise the children. The effects of these verbal attacks should not be underestimated; almost all battered wo-

19

men agree that this abuse is far more devastating than any physical injuries they suffered. As one woman said, "The bruises and cuts would always eventually heal; but the emotional scars never did. I carried them with me all the time." The result of these "psychological beatings" is that the woman herself comes to believe that she could not survive on her own, and that she is a worthless person who simply doesn't deserve any better.

Finally, other family members and well-meaning friends may pressure a woman to remain married "for the sake of the children." Women are often told that if they were really good mothers, they wouldn't deny their children a father. As we shall see, however, the woman who decides to stay on account of her children is making a tragic mistake.

But emotional involvement is not the only reason that women stay in a violent relationship. Economic factors frequently play an important part. Many battered women lack job skills and experience and are therefore incapable of supporting themselves and their children. Even women who are employed still face difficulties. For example, they may not be able to raise the money for the first and last month's rent required by most landlords. If a woman does not work, if her family cannot help her, and if welfare grants are not enough to live on, she may eventually decide that being beaten is the price she must pay for financial survival.

Still another reason that battered women don't leave their husbands is, quite simply, fear. It is quite common for a man to threaten that he will come after his wife and kill her or other family members should she try to leave.

Finally, getting out of a violent relationship is often made more difficult by a lack of community resources. Even if there are shelters or safe houses in the area, these facilities ordinarily operate at full capacity, and a woman may have to wait days or weeks before there is room for her and her children. Many women also find it virtually impossible to obtain legal counsel. The middle class woman is often in a particularly difficult position—her income level makes her ineligible for legal aid and she usually can't afford a private attorney. A problem like this frequently deters women from obtaining restraining orders and filing for separation or divorce.

Corrie

When I interviewed Corrie, I was struck by the fact that she looked much older than her twenty-two years would have suggested. Her face was pale, and she appeared tired and drawn. Dressed in a simple, slightly wrinkled white blouse and a faded red skirt, the person who peered out at me from vacant, brown eyes looked as though she had nearly been defeated by life.

Corrie had been born and raised in Texas. The eldest of eight children, her father was a sharecropper. Although she had been living in California for several years, she had not entirely lost her accent.

"I guess some people'd say that I had it hard. We never had much, but my daddy and momma are good, church goin' people, and there was lots of love in our family. Seein' as I was the oldest, I was always helpin' Momma look after my brothers and sisters. Now, I know some girls like me, who had to care for little ones, grew up sayin' they didn't want no kids at all, 'cause they was sick of 'em. But not me. I loved my family—all of 'em—and one thing I did look forward to was havin' babies of my own. My kids are the best thing I ever had.

I met Joe when I was fourteen. Joe was eighteen, and he was the first boy who ever cared about me. I must say it was real flatterin'. He was a smooth talker, that one. He used to say all sorts of nice things, and crazy me, I believed him. Once we started goin' out, he told everyone that if any other boy ever laid a hand on me, he'd murder him. I believed him, and everybody else did, too, 'cause Joe had a reputation for bein' tough. He was always pickin' fights with someone.

Well, it couldn't have been more than six, eight months before Joe wanted us to go to bed. Now, I'd been taught that that sort of thing was a sin. But Joe had a way of bein' awful convincin'. He said when two people was really in love like us, that God understood and that what we wanted to do was alright. Well, he finally talked me into it. I felt real bad afterwards and I thought for sure he'd dump me off and be with some other girl the next day. But he didn't. He stayed with me. I was glad of that, but you know, things have a way of goin' wrong. About a month later, I found out I was pregnant. At first I thought Joe'd be angry. But when I told him, he said he was glad and wanted to get married. I *was* kinda young to settle down, but there weren't no way I could ask my family to take me. I mean, things was hard enough already. Besides, I *had* been to bed with him, and all. So, I said yes, and we set the date. Now, my momma was real sad. She was sorry to see me, a married woman at the age of fifteen. But I told her it would be one less mouth to feed, and that she was a bride at sixteen and things had worked out okay for her.

Well, everythin' seemed fine until a couple of days before the weddin'. Joe and I was sittin' and talkin' one evenin'. I don't remember why, but somehow we started into an argument. And right in the middle of all this, without no warnin' at all, Joe takes his hand and slaps me across the face. Now, I'd had a switch taken to me when I was young, but never anythin' like that. It made me think twice about spendin' the rest of my life with him. I mean, it's one thing to go beatin' up on other men, but hittin' a woman—well, that's somethin' else again. I was not at all sure I wanted to be Mrs. _____, but I just couldn't see no way out.

Well, Joe showed up the next mornin' all sorry and tellin' me how he couldn't live without me, and how he'd never hit a woman

22

before, and he would never do it again, and how he wanted our baby. And 'cept for that one time, he'd been mostly good to me. And he always took care of his family. See, his daddy deserted 'em when he was little, so soon as he was old enough, Joe went to work. Him and his older brother, Earl, supported his mother and the two younger ones for years. But for all he done for his momma, she didn't appreciate him none. She and Joe didn't get along 'cause she was always sayin' how much he reminded her of his no-good daddy, and how Joe was goin' to turn out bad just like him. Anyway, he seemed so sincere, I just couldn't say 'no.' So, we got married.

After the weddin' Joe dropped out of school to get a fulltime job on a farm. We moved into a little two room house. It wasn't very much, but we were happy—at least at the beginnin'. The whole time I was pregnant, Joe just treated me like a queen. He didn't want me to overdo and he seemed proud of the way I looked. He used to show me off. Well, trouble started soon as that baby came. I had a real hard labor, so I was pretty well exhausted by the time little Johnny came into this world. And it was real tough when he'd cry at night and Joe had to sleep. It made Joe angry—and I could understand—he worked hard all day and he needed a good night's rest. So, I'd walk the floor with the baby and do my best to keep him quiet. See, Johnny was kind of sickly—not real bad, but not quite right, neither. We had these doctor bills start piling up, and pretty soon we was in debt. Well, Joe had to take a second job as a parttime janitor in town, three nights a week. We did okay, but it was awful hard on Joe, and he started drinkin' on weekends to relax.

The worst of it was how he always changed when he was drunk. He's like two different people. When he's sober he can be real nice. He's good to me, tellin' me how much he likes my cookin' and things like that. But when he's been drinkin', he's a real monster. You ever see that television show, "The Incredible Hulk?" That's Joe. When he gets drunk, he can likely pull a door off its hinges. 'Fact, once he tore off our screen door. It jammed when he was tryin' to get out, so he just takes it and he rips it right off. I mean, that's scary, that's scary.

And when Joe was drunk, the kids were afraid of him, too. They'd run and hide. I don't blame 'em. One time, when Johnny was about two, Joe took his belt and spanked him so hard that he had black and blue marks all over his legs and bottom, and I told Joe that if he ever tried that again, I'd take a gun and blow his brains out. 'Cause, it's one thing to beat up on a grown person, but there's no excusin' hittin' on a defenseless little child. Well, after that, Joe never hit any of 'em, but he'd still yell at 'em, call 'em names, and tell 'em how stupid they was. It's no wonder the kids don't like their daddy.

The first time Joe beat me after we was married was when Johnny was about two months old. Joe came in one night real late, and expected me to hop up and fix his supper. I told him 'no,' that Johnny'd just gone to sleep after his two o'clock feedin', that I was tired, and I'd wrapped his dinner and left it in the icebox for him. Well, he didn't take too kindly to that. In fact, what he took was his fist, and he punched me smack in the face. I started cryin' and he grabbed me by the shoulders and he shook me until I thought I'd fall apart. He said, 'You get in there, you little bitch, and you fix your husband some supper like you should.' I wasn't about to argue, but by the time I had it ready, he'd fallen asleep on the couch. He never did eat it. Next mornin', when he saw my cheek all bruised, he said he couldn't believe he'd done that to me. He swore it was just 'cause he'd been drinkin' and he promised he'd cut down. I really couldn't hold it against him. After all, he had an awful lot on him. Here he is, only eighteen and all of a sudden he's got a wife and baby to provide for. And he was still givin' some money to his momma each week.

Well, things went okay for about a year. Then his boss caught him drinkin' on the job and he fired him. I started takin' in some mendin' and laundry to help out. But, you know, seems no matter what I did, about every couple of months he'd be drunk and he'd just pop

24

off and hit me one. It wasn't too bad, really, just some bruises. I'd stay in the house and not see anybody for a few days. I 'specially wanted to keep it from my parents 'cause they'd worry.

Then I found out I was pregnant again. I wasn't surprised—Joe was always after me. I don't know, maybe some men are like that, but so help me every time I'd turn around he wanted me in bed with him. Frankly, I don't see what all the fuss is about. He says it's my wifely duty to satisfy him when and where he wants it, and I suppose he's right. But much as I like babies, I was the one had to carry 'em, and after the first one, Joe wasn't so nice to me. I guess he saw I'd done it once and there weren't nothin' much to it, so I should be able to do it any number of times without too much trouble. Lucky for me our second one, our little girl, wasn't so bad.

Well, after she was born, things got real bad for us. Joe's truck broke down and we had to borrow money to get it fixed. Just seemed we was gettin' deeper and deeper in debt. What's worse, Joe started drinkin' more. I'd get real angry over that. I mean, wastin' good money on beer. He said he needed it to relax, but I told him my daddy never took a drop and he always done just fine.

Joe and I used to have arguments over that. I remember one night he come home drunk and he'd spent nearly all his paycheck on beer. Well, we needed that money, so I really got after him, you know? So he says, 'Woman, you better shut up,' and he hits me right in the mouth. It started bleedin' real bad, so I ran to the bathroom and locked the door. I guess Joe figured he'd got what he wanted, 'cause he went off to bed. Next mornin' my lip was still oozin' blood and looked ugly, so I went to the doctor. After the doctor fixed me up, he said, 'How'd you do this, Corrie?' And I lied. I'm not goin' to tell him I've got a man that beats up on me. So, I said that I tripped and fell on somethin'. He looked at me real suspicious, but he just said, 'You take care.' Well, I didn't speak to Joe for near two days. I couldn't hardly even look at him. I was really beginnin' to think I couldn't live with this man no longer. Then, Joe decided to come out here to California and do construction work like Earl. Joe said he'd stay with Earl and his wife and would make real good pay. Well, we certainly did need the money, 'specially since I was pregnant again. And believe me, I was all for havin' him gone. So, he left for a whole six months. He sent money back pretty regular, and I had my kids and relations to keep me company.

Right after Joe came back, Joe Jr. was born. He was a good, strong, healthy baby, so I was real happy. Then one night Joe walks in and says that we was all movin' to California. He'd already found a place for us out here, near where Earl lived. That was terrible news to me. I'd lived my whole life in Texas, close to my family and all. Movin' this far away just scared me to death. But I was his lawful wife, and it was my duty to go with him. So I packed up everything we owned, said 'good-bye,' and off we went.

Well, turns out comin' here was mostly a bad thing. Joe seemed to be drinkin' an awful lot. He'd stop off after work with Earl and his other buddies, so he come in drunk or close to it almost every evenin'. I think it was 'cause of those construction men. I really do. They was hard drinkers, and they treated their wives like dirt. Joe'd tell me how they all kept women on the side and how they'd fool their wives about it. And Joe started wantin' me to do all these crazy things. He wanted sex a different way every night. No decent woman would ever do some of the things he asked. It just wasn't the way I was raised. He never forced me, except once when he was mighty drunk, but I could tell he was disgusted with me 'cause I couldn't keep up with him and his new set of friends.

'Bout the only good thing out here was meetin' Earl's wife, Nancy. She was a California girl and real nice to me. She worked part-time as a secretary, and she was the independent type—not like me. More 'n once she'd said if Earl didn't lay off her soon, she'd leave him. She was my only real friend out here. She saw the bruises on me from

26

time to time, and finally I just couldn't lie no more. She said the next time it happened I should send Johnny to get the neighbors to call the police.

Well, Nancy seemed pretty smart, you know, so next time he started in on me, I done what she said. I can't say as it did a whole lota good, though. When the police got there, I told 'em, 'Take him away, I never want to see him again.' But since nothin' on me was bleedin', (he hadn't cut me or broken any bones) this policeman says, 'Now calm down. I didn't see it so I can't make an arrest.' I said, 'I don't care. You take him away—you take him away. I want him in jail.' But they just wouldn't take me serious. Well, they did talk him into leaving, and they asked me if I needed to see a doctor or go to the hospital. I said no, I figured nothin' was broken, and that I'd mend. So off they went. When Joe come back, he didn't hit me or nothin', but he said that if I ever so much as *thought* about calling the police again, he'd just as soon kill me as not. And, you know what he said about killin'? Well, it actually come true, just like them prophecies in the Bible.

You see, it wasn't too long before Joe comes in one night drunk and real nasty. Seems Nancy had just told Earl she was goin' to leave him, so him and Joe had gone out drinkin' and talkin', and the more they talked, the angrier they got. So, by the time Joe got home he was in a foul mood. Soon as he come in he started in a-yellin' at me about how horrible Nancy was and how horrible all women was and he used all sorts of words I wouldn't ever repeat. Then he asks me where his dinner is. I mean, it must have been close to eleven o'clock, so I told him it was in the refrigerator. Then he yells at me 'cause the house is kinda messy. Now, he knowed I was pregnant again and that I'd been feelin' real poorly. I'd done the best I could. Well, that just seemed to make him angrier, and he slapped me so hard across the face that I fell to the ground. And then he started kickin' me. I was afraid he'd get me in the face, so I put my arms over my head, but he kicked

27

me in the stomach! I couldn't hardly believe he'd do such a thing, and I screamed at him to stop, that he'd hurt the baby, but he wouldn't stop. He just kept kickin' me. All of a sudden I felt this horrible pain—cramps so awful I just doubled over. Then I started bleedin'. Well, Joe could see he done somethin real bad, but instead of helpin' me he just says, 'Serves you right,' and walks out the door. For awhile I just laid there, cryin'. Of course the kids was up with the noise and all, too scared to come out 'til their daddy left. Well, when they all come in and they saw me layin' there like that, they started cryin', too. I knew I'd have to get to a doctor, so I told Johnny to go call Aunt Nancy. I thank the Lord for Nancy. Anyway, she come right over and took me to the hospital.

The doctor there was real nice. But then he asked me what had happened, and I said I'd fell. He didn't believe me, though, 'cause he asked me again how it had happened. So I said I guessed that God just didn't want this baby to get born. Well, that doctor looked me straight in the eye and he said that God didn't have nothin' to do with it and that the person who done that to me had murdered my baby. Well, that was more than I could take. I just broke down and cried, and I told him everything. And so he tells me after I get out of the hospital that I should leave my husband. I was really pretty lucky 'cause no lastin' harm was done. They gave me somethin' called a 'D and C', and after a few days I was ready to go home.

Well, I'd had lots of time to think, layin' there in that hospital. What that doctor said kept comin' back to me. I decided I couldn't live with no murderer. Besides, even before that horrible night I'd been thinkin' these terrible thoughts, about how nice it'd be if Joe was dead. Fact, a couple of times I even thought of killin' him myself. Now, I'd never had such sinful thoughts before, and it scared me. I prayed about it a long time. I figured I could take livin' with Joe, but I was worried about my kids. It's real hard on them to see their momma get beat up. And I don't want any of them to grow up thinkin' that's the way things is supposed to be. So I done what I had to. When I got out of the hospital, instead of goin' back to Joe, we went and stayed with Nancy. She'd just moved out on Earl, and she said it was fine if we lived there 'til things got settled. That was mighty kind of her, 'cause her place wasn't very big. She helped me go down and apply for welfare. I sure hated doin' that. My daddy ain't never taken a handout, even when times was real bad. But, I just didn't have no choice. You know, life don't always work out the way you want it, and you just got to do the best you can. Anyhow, after about two weeks, I decided I couldn't stay out here no more. Even Joe thinks I belong back home. He says I'm too backward and stupid to make it out here. So, I'm goin'. My daddy said he'd sell one of the hogs and send me the bus fare. I guess it'll come in a week or so. I can't say as I know what's goin' to happen, but my momma and daddy said we'd find some way to manage."

MYTHS

1. IF A WOMAN GETS BEATEN, IT'S PROBABLY BECAUSE SHE DID SOMETHING TO PROVOKE HER HUSBAND.

When a battered woman first tells a friend or relative about her abuse, she's very likely to hear the question: "What did you do to provoke him?" The person who reacts this way not only misunderstands the dynamics of wifebeating, but is also reflecting current societal attitudes about domestic violence. For, the implication of such a question is quite clear—the woman herself is responsible for the violence; if she had behaved in a different manner the beating would never have

29

occurred. Blaming the woman also gives the batterer tacit approval for his violence; it is assumed that a person who is "provoked" has sufficient justification for his actions. Although there are situations in which the woman may also be considered a true combatant, perhaps even landing the first blow herself, such cases are in the minority. In the "battered wife syndrome," the woman is truly a victim. Furthermore, many of the reasons for which women have been beaten are incredibly trivial. Women have been attacked for "provoking" their husbands by not having dinner ready on time, by putting the children to bed too early, by letting the children stay up too late, for wanting to go back to school, and for putting too much salt on the breakfast eggs. One man broke two of his wife's ribs because he didn't like the way she was looking at him.

2. **THE WOMAN WHO IS REALLY SERIOUS ABOUT SOLVING THE PROBLEM COULD JUST HAVE HER HUSBAND ARRESTED AND PUT IN JAIL.**

Although this appears to be a perfectly logical solution, it is neither as simple nor as effective as it might seem. In some states, for example, if a woman's injuries only constitute a misdemeanor, the responding officer cannot make an arrest unless he actually sees the beating in progress. In such cases, if the woman still wants to press charges, she must make a citizen's arrest herself. Even if her husband is taken into custody, he is still eligible to post bail and, depending upon when the arrest is made, he may be released within three or four hours. If the woman has no other place to go, she risks further violence when her spouse returns. I have spoken with many wives who were severely beaten because they had signed complaints against

30

their husbands. Obviously, such an experience would make women reluctant to call the police in the future.

Of course there are some situations when it is to a woman's advantage to have her spouse arrested; if there is a safe place for her to go, she can use the time while he is in custody to pack, gather necessary documents, and make plans. Furthermore, even if police are called and an arrest isn't made, a report can be filed which could later prove to be vital evidence in a civil or criminal proceeding. Nevertheless, even the woman who is "serious" about dealing with the violence cannot simply have her husband or boyfriend arrested and held in jail indefinitely.

Janet

To look at Janet today, one might never suspect that she had experienced the physical and emotional trauma of being a battered woman. When I interviewed her she appeared happy, relaxed, and self-confident. Visibly pregnant, she was dressed in navy blue slacks with a matching blouse. A ruffle at the neck set off her short, neatly combed, brown hair. Her good natured sense of humor and an easy smile bespoke a woman satisfied with herself and her life. But Janet's contentment had been hard-won.

"I guess the thing I remember most about growing up is that there were always restrictions. My father was a minister, and both he and my mother were very concerned with the impression we made. I always had to 'act like a lady,' even at home. To make matters worse, Mom was always afraid I'd get sick or hurt or something. Now, I can understand why my parents were so protective. After all, Mom had had four miscarriages before I was born, and as their only child if something has ever happened to me, well—that would have been it. But I still think they went too far. So help me, I was treated just like a china doll.

My mother and father seemed to think that I might break if I did anything daring or different. I wasn't allowed to date until I was sixteen and even then my father would interrogate the poor boy. Believe it or not, my father opened all my mail, even after I was in college. When I complained about it, he didn't even hear me. He really felt that it was his duty to do it because 'girls needed to be protected.'

For the most part, I went along with the way I was raised. I tried very hard to please my parents and to be a 'good girl.' I had this ideal of being a loving, nurturing, almost saint-like woman. I saw myself as a model wife and mother, spreading peace and love throughout the world. Both my parents and I really looked on a career for me as a stop-gap until I got married. Even then, if I did have to have a job, I was to be a nurse or a teacher or maybe a secretary, although you ran into an awful lot of lecherous men out in the business world.

Even though I usually tried to live up to my parents expectations, I also had quite a stubborn streak. I can remember getting spanked with a hairbrush because even at age three I wanted to fix my hair the way *I* wanted it, and my mother wanted it fixed the way *she* wanted it. The only other time I totally defied my parents, aside from marrying David, was when they decided that it was immoral for a girl to have a two-piece bathing suit. Well, when you're a teenager and your mother wants you to dress like a nineteenth century Victorian with a bathing suit down to your ankles, it's pretty embarrassing. So, without her knowing it, whenever I went off to the beach with some friends, I would go to a girlfriend's house and change into one of her two-piece bathing suits, go to the beach, and change again before going home. I always felt slightly guilty about it, but my girlfriends all said my parents were too old fashioned.

I never really had good communication with my mother and father. Oh, we talked about a lot of superficial things or things that were spiritual, but we never got down to deep feelings. My parents never fought—I don't even remember them ever having an argument

32

in front of me. Anger was simply an emotion you were not supposed to show. Everything in our family had to be discussed calmly and rationally. If you did have a problem or a gripe with someone, you first had to sit down and determine if you were in the right. If it turned out you were in the wrong, then you simply weren't allowed to feel angry. According to my mother and father, you were always supposed to have nice thoughts about people, and if you got angry with someone it was because you were being too proud or too selfish.

And sex. Brother! My mother was so embarrassed when I started to menstruate that she just shoved a book and a box of Kotex at me and said, 'Here, read that. It'll explain everything.' I do remember some general lectures about how all that men wanted was to go to bed with you, and how you had to be so careful to keep your virtue. It was also made very clear that sex was a duty for wives and that women weren't really supposed to enjoy it. We were to do it to please our husbands and to have children, but that was all. To give you an idea of my mother's attitude, one day when I was little, she had caught me playing with myself—like all kids do. Well, this absolutely horrified her. She called it 'self-abuse.' I don't think she could, even to this day, use the term 'masturbate.' It's simply not in her vocabulary. At any rate, she was really angry and gave me a terrible spanking. She told me if I kept it up it would ruin my health and maybe even lead to insanity. It's hard to imagine anyone being that 'backward,' but that was the way she had been raised. For the most part, I believed her. After all, I was only five or six years old. The end result of all this was that when I did finally start dating I was quite naive and almost afraid of boys. I had plenty of social graces but I didn't know a thing about the real world. And I often think that if my parents had not tried to protect me so much, I might not have made the mistake of marrying David.

I met David in high school. He had a reputation as a 'ladies man.' He was good looking, charming, and athletic. The first time he asked me for a date, I was flabbergasted. I never would have guessed

33

that such a popular boy would ever want to take me out. David could have had his pick of any of the girls, and I just wasn't the social butterfly type that he usually went around with. When I graduated at seventeen and entered a local college we continued to see each other. He was the first man who really took an interest in me, and he was always an absolute gentleman. But he was also kind of jealous of me. He let it be known that I was his girl and no one else was supposed to lay a hand on me. I was flattered by all this attention, and quite willing to mold my behavior to his desires. He had already begun work as a junior salesman, and was awfully good at it—David could charm the pants off of anybody—so he usually had money to spend and we would go to nice places. He just swept me off my feet. There is just no other way to describe it.

It wasn't too long before I was sure I had met 'prince charming.' My 'knight in shining armor' had arrived and this was going to be love eternal. My parents were not pleased. They thought we were too young and that he didn't come from a good enough family for me. David's father had never finished college, but he had become a successful building contractor, and his mother worked part-time as a secretary for her husband. David was the baby of the family—the youngest child and only boy with three older girls. Even as an adult, he was somewhat spoiled by his sisters and mother and he was used to getting just about anything he wanted.

When I turned eighteen and I knew I could do exactly what I wanted, I went ahead and married David. I think now that it was almost as much an act of rebellion as an act of really wanting to get married. But at the time I didn't see any of that. To me it was the chance to fulfill a dream, and I was sure marriage would be pure heaven. I was going to live happily ever after in our house in the suburbs with 2.7 children, a station wagon, membership in the PTA, and bridge on Thursday. I also wanted a chance to have my 'own place'—that had been a dream of mine, too—to finally be out on my own. I would still be safe, though, because David was there to take care of me. I really just transferred my dependency on Mommy and Daddy to David.

Well, my heavenly match only lasted about two years. At that time I discovered I was pregnant. We were living in a nice little apartment and David was doing all right in his work. I was delighted to find out that I was going to have a baby. I was so excited, I could hardly wait to tell Dave the news when he came home that evening. Well, he was less than pleased. At first he didn't even react at all, so I pressed him for some kind of an answer. 'Aren't you happy? Aren't you excited that you're going to be a father? Don't you think it's wonderful?' All I got out of him was, 'Yeah, yeah, but it's going to be expensive.' I was really disappointed, but I kind of shrugged it off, thinking, 'Well, he's young yet. This will be a bit responsibility for him. He'll feel differently later.'

Things went pretty well until I was about six months pregnant. David had presumably adjusted to the idea of being a father, and even took some pride in the fact that here was this pregnant woman that he, virile David, had made that way. It was a great sign of his manhood. I really thought that everything would be fine. Boy, was I ever wrong. See, David liked to go out with his buddies a lot and I was never invited along—that was a man's activity. I had really begun to get tired of being left at home. One evening we were arguing about it and I could see him getting angrier and angrier. Suddenly, without warning, he slapped me across the face. I was absolutely dumbfounded. I just couldn't believe that anyone would ever do anything like that. David was immediately sorry. He said that he'd had to do it to bring me to my senses because I was getting hysterical. Well, dumb little old me, I believed him. I guess my reaction was really just to deny it all. In fact, by the next morning I had succeeded in convincing myself that the whole incident had been my fault, and that it really wasn't worth even thinking about. It was just as if I had constructed a dream world for myself and I wasn't going to let anything destroy it.

35

There were no more incidents until about three months after Timmy was born. David seemed to resent the amount of time that I had to spend with the baby. For my part, I kind of liked being a mother, but I did feel a bit trapped. David started going out in the evenings more and more. He and 'the boys' went to bars or over to someone's house to sit around and drink beer. It really became an issue. One night in particular he had gone out and come back pretty drunk. He made so much noise when he came in that he woke the baby, who naturally started crying. For some reason, I just couldn't seem to get Timmy to quiet down and go back to sleep. This made David very angry. He wanted his household run to suit him, and a noisy baby was not something that he wanted to hear. After a few minutes of trying to get Timmy to be quiet, I began to get a little angry myself. After I determined that he wasn't hungry and he was dry, I put Timmy back in his crib and decided I'd just have to let him cry it out. When I came back into the livingroom, the first thing David said was, 'Can't you get that damn baby to shut up?' I said no, I couldn't, he would just have to listen to him cry. Then David came at me. I can still re- member that wild look in his eyes. I had never seen it before and it really frightened me. He said something like, 'You bitch, you'd better keep him quiet,' and he grabbed me by the arm and threw me up against the wall. He had me pinned to the wall and was slapping me in the face again and again. I started crying and screaming at him to stop it. That just seemed to make him angrier and he threw me to the floor. I started to get up and he came over to me and gave me a kick in the side as if to say, 'There, you're down; I've asserted myself.' Then he stomped out of the apartment. I just lay there and cried for awhile. I couldn't move; I didn't want to move. Finally I dragged myself up and went into the baby's room and got him a bottle. Even- tually he went back to sleep. I just sat in the rocking chair and rocked for the longest time. I couldn't seem to think straight. About two hours later, David came back. I guess he'd sobbered up or something, because he was really shocked at what he had done. He said that he was truly sorry, that he'd just been drinking too much, and that it would never happen again. He begged me to forgive him. He said how much he loved me and Timmy and that he would be lost without us. He told me he just didn't know what had come over him—that he never intended to hurt me at all. I honestly didn't know what to think, but I did so want to believe him. The next day he brought me flowers and he took me out to dinner. It was easy for me to tell myself that the violence was due to the drinking and that he really did care for me and the baby. He seemed so sincere that I thought things might be all right after all.

Well, as it turned out, things were far from all right. Over the next year and a half our relationship just got worse and worse. It seemed that as Timmy got older, Dave became more demanding of my time, and more rigid in his expectations. He'd get angry if I wasn't there when he got home from work, and he wanted dinner exactly on time—not a minute later. I do think he loved Timmy and I guess he tried to be a good father to him. But he was always trying to get Timmy to do more than he was able. Dave liked to roughhouse with him and Timmy usually thought that was fun. Once, though, he was tossing him up in the air and catching him and Tim got scared and started to cry. Well, this irritated David because he was sure his son was going to grow up to be a crybaby and a sissy. So he just shoved him into my arms and stamped out of the house.

All during this period I was walking on eggs, doing everything I could to keep from irritating him so that he wouldn't get angry. But no matter what I did he'd haul off and hit me about once every couple of months. He always said that he was sorry and I always forgave him. David and I didn't talk much anymore. He had never been very verbal, but now all we could do was exchange a few superficial remarks. He also started to call me names and criticize the way I kept house and the way I looked. This was totally different from the David I had married.

At the beginning, he couldn't say enough good things about me. But now he complained that I'd become a frumpy old housewife, that I didn't keep myself up, and that I wasn't as good a housekeeper as his mother who, after all, had had four children and not just one baby to look after. So I tried even harder, but nothing I did was ever quite good enough. I became very depressed. It got to be an effort just to do my everyday chores.

Our sexual relationship got worse, too. Sex had been pretty good with David, even though I never had an orgasm. But for someone who was raised to think that sex was terrible, I guess it wasn't so bad. Sometimes after he was violent and had come back and apologized, he would want to take me to bed. He said he wanted to make up, but I really think this was just his way of getting rid of his own guilt. After all, if I made love to him, he'd figure that all was forgiven and we could go on as if nothing had happened. Most of the time, though, I could hardly bear for him to touch me after a beating. I explained that to him once and he really surprised me by saying, 'That's okay. I understand,' and he left me alone that night. As time went on, I found it more and more difficult to respond to him even if he hadn't been violent. I knew better than to refuse him too often, though, so I just pretended that I liked it.

I was terribly unhappy during that time in my life, but I simply didn't see how I could leave, because I had no way to support Timmy and myself. Besides, I was determined to make the marriage work regardless of what it took. I'll tell you, though, if I had had any idea what was in store for me, I would have left right then. Up until then, David had confined his violence to slapping and shoving. But then things took a turn for the worse.

One night he came home drunk after some party. I made the mistake of saying something about his drinking and I asked him to be quiet because of the baby. That made him angry. He accused me of loving Timmy more than I loved him and we went through the routine

38

of how inadequate I was as a woman. I started to defend myself with all sorts of explanations, but I could see that I wasn't getting anywhere, so I told him to go sleep it off—that I just didn't want to talk with him when he was drunk. He refused to leave, so I started for the bedroom. He shouted at me to come back and talk to him—that he was still the man of the house and I had better do what he said. Stupidly, I didn't take him seriously, and I kept on walking. He grabbed me by the arm and turned me around. When I saw his face, I was absolutely horrified. It was as if some mad man had come in and taken over his body. Then I saw his fist coming toward me. The next thing I remember was lying on the floor with David crying over me and putting a cold cloth on my eye. My eye was swollen shut and I felt sick at my stomach. I started crying and asking him, 'What did you do to me? What did you do to me? How could you do such a thing?' I wanted to go into the bathroom and clean up or something, but he didn't want me to see myself, I guess. He helped me into bed and left me alone.

When I woke up in the morning (he let me sleep late for a change) he'd already gone to work. I got up to take care of Timmy and I saw myself in the mirror. It was beyond words. My eye was still swollen and red and the whole side of my face seemed bruised. At that point I knew I couldn't take anymore. I simply couldn't go on. Up until then I hadn't told anyone about the violence, especially my mother and father. But it had gotten so bad I figured I'd take the risk and talk to my parents. My mother was terribly upset by it all, but her question to me was, 'What did you do to make David act like that?' I tried to explain, but I don't think she ever understood. All in all, my parents were pretty good about it. They were sorry I'd been though all that and said it was inexcusable. However, their advice was for me and David to go to church more often. I knew that would never happen because David's mother used to drag him around to church when he was a kid and he hated it. I was also supposed to forgive my husband because that was the Christian thing to do, and we would all pray for him to change. I must say that that was one of the lowest days in my entire life. I was frightened, confused, and depressed. I felt so completely alone. I was sure that I was the only woman in the world who was beaten and I was also sure I would never find anyone who really understood what I was going through. It was just as though a wave of hopelessness had swept over me and there was no way in the world that I could ever be happy again.

When I got back home I found that David had cleaned up the house, something which he would ordinarily never do. Timmy had been fed and was sleeping, and except for the fact that I looked so terrible, he acted as if nothing was wrong. I really think he expected me to forgive him and to go on as if things were just fine between us. I was pretty much resigned to my fate and decided to try to make the best of the situation. However, it was very hard to cope. David became more vicious in his attacks on me verbally and more frequent in his violence. I later found out that he had begun having an affair with his secretary. He hadn't touched me sexually in six months and though I didn't understand why at the time, I wasn't complaining. I was glad that he left me alone.

I was basically miserable but I can understand now why I stayed so long. You see, David was always apologetic and told me he needed my help. That brought out the 'Florence Nightingale' in me. I was going to save this poor suffering man and turn him into, if not a saint, then certainly a happy, well-adjusted person. And I was sure I could do it. I had been brought up believing that 'love conquers all,' and since everybody knew that I was this loving person, everything would work out all right eventually. For awhile there, I really thought I was quite virtuous to take so much punishment for the good of another person. I had sort of convinced myself that what I was doing was noble, and that somehow I would be rewarded. This grand illusion of mine kept me going pretty well. Also, I was fortunate that Sarah, a divorcee, and her little girl moved in next door. She and I became very good friends. I never told her about the violence directly but we did talk about other problems. After some time, she convinced me to go back to school, even if I only took one course. She was working parttime and going to school, too. I could see that she managed very well and I figured if she could do it, I could do it, too. I had always been a good student so I felt I could handle it. Besides, Timmy was three years old then and going to a nursery school in the morning. I had liked school and I thought that maybe this would be a way to make me happy. Well, when I asked David if I could do it, his answer was a flat 'no.' He said that I would be spending more time away, and that I already wasn't able to take care of the house or him or the child well enough. How could I possibly expect to do all that and go to school, too? Well, this upset me. I didn't want to spend the rest of my life at home with kids. I told him I would only go parttime, but that didn't satisfy him. Finally, after begging and pleading, I got him to agree to let me take one class. That was a mistake. He never forgave me for 'winning' that argument and I paid dearly for getting my way.

Being in school created friction between us but I tried extra hard to keep the house nice and cook good meals. Things went pretty well until one night when I stopped off after class to have coffee with a woman friend. This made me about a half hour late getting home. When I got home, I found that David was there already. He had taken the sitter home and he was waiting for me. Well, the moment I walked in the door, he was at me—wanting to know where I had been and accusing me of being out with a man. Every denial I made just seemed to make him angrier. I could see that horrible look coming in his eyes and I knew that meant trouble so I tried to get away by going in the other room. It didn't work. He grabbed me and started punching me with his fists. I started screaming, and then Timmy came in and *he* started screaming and crying. We were making such a ruckus, I was really surprised the neighbors didn't hear or come or do anything but they never did. Timmy tried to grab him and pull him off, but David

41

just brushed him aside. He pushed me to the ground and began kicking me. I put my arms over my head to protect myself. It was just like a nightmare. I heard Timmy screaming and David screaming. I was so frightened and in so much pain that I thought, 'If he kicks me one more time, I'm just going to give up and die.' I figured I had just about had it when he suddenly stopped. To this day I don't know what made him stop but he did. Then he stomped out of the house. I could barely move. Every place I could feel hurt. I knew that that was it—I just couldn't take any more. By sheer force of will I got up and pulled myself together. I packed my clothes and Timmy's things and went to the only place that I could—back to my parents.

At first, they were somewhat reluctant to have me stay with them. They thought that a woman's place was with her husband and that they would be contributing to the breakup of a marriage. At that point I became hysterical. I just broke down and sobbed and sobbed, so they finally let us stay there. I was with my parents for about a week. I was away from Dave, which was nice, but it was no picnic. I got the third degree about my life and what had happened to me. Naturally, Dave put on the 'I'm sorry' act. He showed up at my parents house every day, begging me to come back. He sent flowers. He sent letters. He phoned. He told me that I was the most beautiful and most wonderful woman in the whole world. He said he didn't deserve me— I'll have to agree with that—and that he would get counseling if only I would come back. He also said I could go back to school. He claimed he was serious about being a good husband and he begged me not to break up the family. Well, between him and my parents and my own doubts, I decided to go back and give it one more try.

For about four or five months, things really went well. David even went to see a counselor. He said he was going every week. I later found out that he had only gone twice. But I didn't know that at the time and besides, being in school again made me very happy. I also began talking to a counselor. I didn't say anything about the violence but she did help me to become a little more assertive. I started asking questions about why things were the way they were. Why couldn't I handle some of the money? Why couldn't I be involved in more decision-making? Naturally, this bothered Dave. He thought I was becoming too independent.

During this last period with him, while he was supposedly going to counseling, we started having sex again. But I really think too much bad had happened between us because it was never good for me again. In fact, the next really big incident was over sex. He had been out with the boys again and I had gone to bed. I guess it was around midnight when he came in and he wanted to make love. Well, I was really tired. I'd been in class all day and had done all the laundry besides. So, I said no, and just rolled over. That made him so angry he became like a mad man. He came at me and I thought he was going to choke me. But instead of grabbing my throat, he took the neck of my nightgown and literally ripped it off of me. He came after me, yelling 'You bitch, when I want to screw, we're going to screw.' He dragged me back into the bedroom and threw me on the bed. I was scared but I was angry, too. So when he tried to get on top of me, I kicked him in the stomach. If I had hit him lower, I think he might have killed me. Unfortunately, that blow just made him angrier. He slapped me across the face two or three times and pinned my arms to the bed. Then he jumped on me. I can still remember what it was like. It hurt like hell and it seemed to go on forever. When he finally finished with me, he simply rolled over and fell asleep. I got up and took a shower. I felt dirty inside and out. Then I sat up the rest of the night thinking. I would never have thought a wife could be raped by her own husband but I believe it now.

After that, I knew that I could never stay married to him. I had to get out for good. I didn't have a job and I hadn't finished school. So, I thought of ways I might be able to save money out of the household account, or perhaps even borrow some money from my father. I really made some careful plans. As it turned out, however, I

43

never got to use those plans because the issue was forced the very next day. The next morning at breakfast we barely exchanged but a couple of words. But that afternoon, just like the script said, he came in with flowers and said he was really sorry. This time the scene was really spectacular. When I told him I wasn't interested in his apologies anymore, he fell down on his knees and started to cry. I couldn't believe what I was seeing. But I was determined to hold my ground, and I kept telling him that apologies were no good, that it was all over. Then he pulled a new one on me. He said that he would commit suicide if I ever left him. My first reaction was, 'Oh, oh, I certainly don't want *that* on my conscience.' But on second thought, I was so sick and tired of the whole thing, I just said, 'Go ahead, do it.' But then he said, 'Okay, you can watch me kill myself and I'm going to take Timmy with me.' And he headed off for the closet where the gun was kept. Well, I just couldn't take any chances. God, I mean, I could just see him blowing both their heads off. Timmy was out playing in the front yard, so I grabbed him by the arm and we ran like crazy next door to Sarah's, and pounded the hell out of her door. Luckily she was home and she let us in. About a minute later, David caught up with us. He began banging on the door and shouting that he'd shoot the lock off if I didn't come out immediately. Well, Sarah was fantastic. She told him that if he didn't leave she'd call the police. Well, he ranted and raved for a little while, then I guess he gave up. Timmy and I spent the night with Sarah. She and I sat and talked for the longest time. I told her *everything*. It really felt good to finally get all that off my chest.

The next day, with Sarah's help I found a lawyer, filed for divorce, got a restraining order, and sort of girded myself to withstand all the criticism that I knew was coming. And was I ever right! David agreed to move out, but he made it clear that it wasn't his choice and that he wanted me back. He was the perfect martyr. He told everyone what a terrible person I was to leave him when he needed me and loved me so much. He blamed me for breaking up a ten year marriage and a perfectly happy family. I got pressure from all over—my family, him, his family—they all told me I was making a big mistake. David hounded me constantly, calling me all the time. I kept hanging up on him so much that he finally got tired of it and turned to writing letters instead. I got one almost every day. Sometimes, he'd be angry, sometimes forgiving, sometimes remorseful. At least he didn't come by very often. We had the house up for sale and all I would have needed was to have had a scene while some prospective buyer was there.

I was really determined to make a new life for myself and for Timmy. I was lucky to have a counselor at school who I could talk to. She helped me get a parttime job at the university day care center. I rented a small, one bedroom apartment, and just barely managed to make ends meet. Sometimes it was hard being out on my own, especially when Timmy was sick or when I couldn't pay all the bills. It seemed as if David was always late with the child support payments. But all in all, I was much happier than I had been with David. It was wonderful having the freedom to do what I wanted when I wanted and knowing that I didn't always have to be on my guard, wondering when the next attack would come. Timmy improved, too. He had always been tense and had had trouble sleeping. Well, he just calmed down amazingly without his father around. My relationship with him got much better. I had less time with him now that I was working and going to school, but when I did get home I could really relax and enjoy being with him. Before, it seemed like so much of my energy was taken up just trying to cope with David, I didn't have much left to give to Timmy.

I was also very lucky because about eight months after the divorce, I met Paul. I was immediately attracted to him, and we started dating. But I was still afraid. I even tried to push him to the limit to see if he would lose control and hit me. We had some real yelling matches but he never touched me. After we had been dating for awhile, he asked me to move in with him, and I thought that would be a good idea so I would be extra sure that he was the right man for me. This, of course, mortified my parents, but I am pleased to say that I was able to withstand all that. I lived with Paul for about six months and then we got married. We have been married for three years now and I'm happier than I ever thought I would be. I was able to graduate and I got a B.A. in child development. And, as you can see, our baby is due in three months.

Strange to say, the experience of being able to get out of a violent situation has been a positive one, I think. I really like myself now, and I don't think I ever did before. I'm still not entirely over it, though. Sometimes I have nightmares. I see David like a spectre at my bedroom window, haunting and menacing, as if the memory of him and what happened will never leave me. It's so real and so scary, it sometimes wakes me up. But then I see Paul lying there next to me, and I remind myself that my life with David *is* just a bad dream now."

MYTHS

1. MOST BATTERED WOMEN GREW UP IN FAMILIES WHERE THERE WAS VIOLENCE.

Studies indicate that less than half of the women who are battered were exposed to violence as they were growing up. Many abused women came from "nice, respectable" families where daughters were overprotected and sheltered from unpleasant realities. This overprotection, while well intentioned, can later contribute to a woman's inability to effectively cope with a batterer. Such a woman is likely to believe that "this sort of thing" just doesn't happen, and that she alone is married to a violent man. She may therefore conclude that she is indeed to

46

blame for the abuse. In addition to being overprotected, these women were also frequently taught to supress or control any negative emotions. When a woman who has been raised with this attitude reacts with justified anger to a beating, she may feel very guilty about her feelings and turn the anger inward instead of dealing with it in a more constructive manner. This frequently causes physical disorders, such as ulcers, and can also lead to depression. If a woman never sees her parents argue, she may conclude that couples always get along well, and that it is her duty to keep the waters smooth. Of course, it is not beneficial for children to grow up in a home where there is constant discord and quarreling. Ideally, a child should see that parents do disagree, can argue, and can come to reasonable and mutually satisfying solutions without resorting to violence.

Finally, battered women were usually also brought up according to a traditional sex role model; they were expected to be dependent, submissive, and to see their main function in life as being a wife and mother. Later, these women tend to believe that they have primary responsibility for making the marriage a success. Since divorce is viewed as a personal failure, they feel they must keep the relationship together at all costs.

2.   IF A BATTERED WOMAN REMARRIES, SHE WILL USUALLY CHOOSE ANOTHER VIOLENT MAN.

This statement reflects the misconception that battered women need or like the abuse, and will, therefore, consciously or subconsciously, seek out another wifebeater. Although a woman may choose a succession of two or even three violent men, this is usually the exception rather than the rule. The majority of women with whom I have had contact said that

47

although it had been difficult learning how to trust again, they had been able to establish stable, loving, mutually satisfying relationships with their current husbands. Although I certainly do not recommend living with violence as a means of achieving personal growth, it is important to note that many of the women I interviewed said they felt that their experiences with a batterer had made them stronger. As one woman put it, "I really believe that if I could get through *that*, I could get through *anything*." Even women who had not received professional counseling often reported that they had developed a new sense of self worth, independence, and competence. Of course, there are also women who find it difficult or impossible to overcome their feelings of bitterness and mistrust.

But in spite of the success of many second marriages, the effects of having been physically abused should not be underestimated. Once a woman has been battered, she tends to become sensitized to any implied threat of violence, and she can overreact to even innocent gestures. One woman described an incident in which her present non-violent spouse had playfully put his hands at her neck. At that point she became hysterical, and started flailing wildly. The next thing she remembered was huddling in a corner, crying. This woman had not experienced any abuse for *nine years*.

CHAPTER II

HISTORICAL PRECEDENTS FOR WIFEBEATING

Wifebeating has been an accepted practice in Western culture since the early Middle Ages. In fact, it is only recently that society has begun to challenge the longstanding tradition which gives a man both the moral and legal right to batter his spouse.

Throughout history there have been legal, economic, religious and cultural factors which have contributed to the incidence of wife abuse. For example, wifebeating may be perpetuated by statutes which sanction violence against women or which prohibit them from taking legal action against their husbands. Women who are denied full economic opportunities find it harder—if not impossible—to survive financially without a husband, and religions which view woman's subordinate position as divinely ordained make social change and progress difficult. Cultural conceptions of femininity not only influence the relative overall social status of women, but also effectively control behavior through the process of socialization; women who are brought up to believe that they are weak, incompetent, and helpless are less likely to challenge existing restrictions.

The Middle Ages

During the Middle Ages the influence of Christianity should

have theoretically improved the status of women; Jesus' teachings were egalitarian and did not contain the misogyny found in Judaism.[1] However, the writings of the early saints reflected a basic mistrust of women.[2] There were at least two major reasons for the Medieval Church's negative attitudes toward women. First, the Christian religion had incorporated many Jewish beliefs about the nature of the female sex. For example, in the narrative of "The Fall," it was made clear that Eve was entirely to blame for the fact that mankind had been expelled from the idyllic Garden of Eden. During the Middle Ages this was loosely interpreted as meaning that woman was responsible for all the evil and sin in the world.[3] Furthermore, Eve's transgression provided justification for keeping all women in a subordinate social position. I have always found it interesting that Adam himself never took any real responsibility for his own actions. Instead, he maintains that it was Eve's fault: "The woman whom thou gavest to be with me, she gave me fruit of the tree and I ate" (Genesis 3:12). Presumably, Adam possessed free will, and certainly could have refused the offer. But, then, that is not the "stuff" of which patriarchies are made.

Religious prejudice against women was also the result of the attitudes of the Church founders.[4] To them, women primarily represented a temptation to succumb to carnal desires, thereby impeding spiritual growth. For example, the writings of Saint Paul reflect considerable ambivalence toward women. In Galatians he states: "There is neither Jew nor Greek, there is neither bond nor free, there is neither male nor female: for ye are all one in Christ Jesus" (3:28). In Ephesians, however, St. Paul writes: "Wives, be subject to your husbands, as to the Lord . . . As the Church is subject to Christ, so let wives also be subject in everything to their husbands" (5:22-3).

The feelings about women expressed by early saints were echoed by the clergy of the high Middle Ages. Marbode, an eleventh century bishop, said this of women: "Of all the numberless snares that the crafty enemy (the devil) spreads for us. . .the worst. . .is woman, sad stem, evil root, vicious fount. . .honey and poison."[5] However, such passages can be misleading unless one closely examines the context in which they were written. For example, Marbode's diatribe was primarily in reference to prostitutes. When speaking of the matron, he changed his language considerably, stating: ". . .the worst woman who ever lived does not compare with Judas and the best man does not equal Mary."[6] However, the Church generally viewed women as simple creatures, incapable of higher spiritual or intellectual achievement. Women were physically and morally weak, and therefore, justly placed under the total control of fathers and husbands.[7]

But if the Church were somewhat equivocal in assessing the relative merit of the female sex, the clergy clearly believed that a husband had the right, sometimes even the obligation, to beat his wife. In Friar Cherubino's "Rules of Marriage," he states that if a husband's verbal correction of his wife were not effective, then he was to ". . . take up a stick and beat her soundly, for it is better to punish the body and correct the soul than to damage the soul and spare the body. . . then readily beat her, not in rage, but out of charity and concern for her soul, so that the beating will redound to your merit and her good."[8] Just how many women were bruised and battered out of their husbands' sense of Christian charity and duty, we shall never know.

The Medieval Church's attitude toward women, however, was not entirely negative; at least women were viewed as possessing souls worth saving, and marriage was considered a sacrament instituted by Christ.[9] Furthermore, there were some clerics who disapproved of violence, and spoke out strongly against it.[10] Nevertheless, the consensus among the clergy was that a husband was justified in beating his wife.

The subjection of women to physical abuse was also sanctioned by secular institutions. One thirteenth century French law code stated that, "In a number of cases men may be excused for the injuries they inflict on their wives, nor should the law intervene. Provided he neither

51

kills nor maims her, it is legal for a man to beat his wife if she wrongs him."[11] The laws of Gascony included the following statute: "Every inhabitant of this village has the right to beat his wife provided that death does not follow."[12]

Although wives were not protected by law from violence, they did have some legal rights. In England and on the Continent, women, married or single, could hold land, own goods, make wills and contracts, sue and be sued.[13] However, a woman could not appear in court without her husband, and by no means was she considered to be a full citizen; a woman's husband was still her lord in almost every sense of the word.

During the Middle Ages, there were conflicting norms regarding the proper treatment of noble women. The Chivlric code admonished men to serve and honor all women,[14] but physical abuse of wives in the upper class was quite acceptable. For example, the "Book of the Knight of La Tour-Landry," a very popular manual, described the duties and customs of upper class society. One of the stories in this book recounted the misfortunes of a wife who made the mistake of scolding her husband in public. This effontery made him so angry that he, ". . .smote her with his fist down to the earth and then with his foot struck her in the face and broke her nose which all of her life after she had her nose crooked."[15] Wives also had far less freedom in their love affairs than did their husbands. Men from all social classes customarily had mistresses, a practice which was generally condoned. However, if a woman dared to commit adultery—and was caught—she was publicly disgraced, and her lover could be castrated or killed.

The societal view of lower class women appears to have been more uniformly unflattering. In the earthy "fabliaux," short stories about peasant life, these wives were depicted as adulterous, ill-tempered shrews, dedicated to making the lives of their husbands miserable.[16] In these account, the man usually becomes so frustrated with his wife that he occasionally beats her. However, it is also implied that she always has the last word, and that the beatings have little effect on her behavior. The portrait of the scolding wife provoking her mate to violence justly deserved, is a myth which still exists today.

Generally speaking, medieval society viewed women as needing strict control: "The female is an empty thing, easily swayed: she runs great risks when she is away from her husband. Therefore, keep females in the house, keep them as close to you as you can, and come home often to keep an eye on your affairs and to keep them in fear and trembling. . .If you have a female child, set her to sewing and not to reading, for it is not suitable for a female to know how to read unless she is going to be a nun. . ."[17]

Although women had only limited legal rights and almost no political power, they were active in industry, and the growth of towns tended to increase women's freedoms. Many women were traders, and played an important part in the economy of London. Women were also prominent in cloth and silk making, and could usually become members of guilds. Even though women were ordinarily paid less for the same work than men,[18] their labors could often net substantial income. In the area of economics, at least, women were considered to be productive, valuable members of society.

Nevertheless, life for the Medieval woman was primarily one of subjection to the male members of her family. And, although society was slowly beginning to grant her some rights and privileges, she was still provided little, if any, protection from a violent spouse.

Renaissance and Reformation (1400 to 1700)

The Renaissance and Reformation were periods of extraordinary social, political, and religious change. The status of women was changing, too. For the first time higher education was advocated for women, although initially only for those of the upper class.[19] However, there was still some uncertainty about the proper role for a woman.

The Elizabethan wife was, "A curious mixture of slave and companion, a necessary evil, and a valued lieutenant."[20] According to custom, a wife's primary duty was subject to her husband; she was always to acknowledge herself as an inferior, and be ready at the beck and call of her spouse. A husband was to love his wife, to govern her, and to maintain himself in the superior position which God intended him to occupy.[21]

A more intimate view of married life during the Renaissance is provided by the diary of a fourteenth century Florentine merchant. For example, he wrote that he was careful to express disapproval of "bold females" who tried to know about things outside the house. He also took pains to maintain his dominance at all times. "Never, at any moment, did I choose to show in word or action the least self-surrender in front of my wife. I did not imagine for a moment that I could hope to win obedience from one to whom I had confessed myself a slave. Always, therefore, I showed myself virile and a real man."[22]

The Protestant Reformation brought both progress and problems for women. On the one hand, there was a revitalized emphasis on the dignity and spirituality of marriage. More important, a couple was justified in seeking a divorce if their relationship did not allow for the spiritual growth of both partners. For example, one Dominican monk wrote that, "In all things that pertain to salvation, one should have as much regard for a woman as for a man. For though she is bound to keep her place, to put herself under the authority of her husband. . . her subjection does not cancel the right of an honest woman, in accordance with the laws of God, to have recourse to and demand, by legitimate means, deliverance from a husband who hates her."[23] In practice, however, obtaining a divorce through civil courts or through the Church was extremely difficult, and conditions did not substantially improve for several hundred years. Furthermore, even in the new Protestant sects, women were not allowed much authority. In short, neither Catholic nor Protestant leadership was yet ready to grant women full equality with men.

Although women were becoming more educated and had a certain degree of freedom during the Renaissance and Reformation, the reaction to these changes was not entirely positive. In 1620, for example, King James became so annoyed at the presumption of women to copy men's dress and to cut their hair, that he urged the clergy to take the matter promptly in hand. Not surprisingly, the impropriety of women who would take on men's clothes—and men's roles—soon became the topic of sermons throughout England.[24]

But perhaps the most disturbing and malevolent phenomenon during the sixteenth and seventeenth centuries was witch hunting. The belief in witches was held by uneducated and educated alike. The most authoritative and popular work on demonology, the "Maleus Maleficarum," was written around 1486 in Germany. According to this book, the devil found it easier to seduce women than men because the female sex was more feeble in both mind and body. But the primary reason women became witches was said to be because of their "insatiable" carnal lust.[25] The persecution of witches was presumably based on Biblical injunctions, but some of the anti-feminism may well have been in reaction to the growth of women's rights which had been occurring. Whatever the reasons, many innocent people suffered; between 1587 and 1593, for instance, twenty-two villages in the region of Trier burned 368 supposed witches. In 1577 alone, Toulouse and its environs reportedly burned 400 women.[26] Although witch hunting had peaked by the second half of the sixteenth century, the practice continued for another hundred years.

During the Renaissance a bias against women was also evident in the legal system. In England, for example, a man could beat an outlaw, a traitor, a pagan, his servant, or his wife without fear of punishment. Women thus mistreated had no recourse but to pray God would send them ". . .better sport or better company."[27] Nevertheless, some progress was being made, and by the time of King James' reign, (1603-

1625), some judges had expressed the opinion that a wife might take action against her husband for "unreasonable correction." Under Charles II, at least one judge held that moderate castigation was to be understood as meaning a verbal admonition only. However, many other jurists still maintained that a husband had the right to beat his wife as long as he did not do it "outrageously." The Common Law of Wales allowed a man to beat a disrespectful wife three strokes with a rod the length of his forearm and the thickness of his middle finger.[28] And, in 1632, in a methodical collection of statutes and customs entitled, "The Lawes Resolutions of Women Right: or, The Lawes Provision for Woemen(sic)," the author's learned opinion was that husbands indeed had the right to beat their wives but, in fact, should not use it.[29]

As during the Middle Ages, women played an active role in the economy of the Renaissance and Reformation. Trade guilds appear to have been open to girls who had to earn their own livelihood, and marriage to a member of a guild conferred rights upon the wife. A woman could also retain these rights after her husband's death. Women managed ale houses, were innkeepers, worked as upholsterers, milliners, and were sometimes paid for being wet, dry, and sick nurses.[30]

During the Renaissance, women who stayed in their proper place as obedient wives or lovers—when wanted—were treated with some praise and reverence. However, when women tried to assume other responsibilities and roles, they were commonly met with scorn.[31] And, although women did gain some judicial support, they still enjoyed little actual protection from violent husbands.

Early Modern Period, England and France (1700 to 1800)

By the beginning of the eighteenth century, women had achieved a number of legal, moral, and spiritual rights. However, during the eighteen hundreds, legal changes occurred which actually left women with fewer prerogatives than they had had during the Middle Ages. The cause of this was a theory known as "couverture." As explained by Blackstone in his *Commentaries on the Law of England*, it was a custom or law which held that, "In marriage the husband and wife are one person in law; that is the very being or legal existence of the woman is suspended during the marriage, or at least incorporated and consolidated into that of her husband; under whose wing, protection, and cover, she performs everything."[32] The net effect of "couverture" was that a married woman could not own property, have money in her name, control her wages if she worked, make contracts, sue or be sued in court.[33] This latter restriction had particular application to violence; a woman could not prosecute her husband for beating her because in the "eyes of the law" she simply did not exist. Single women, however, were treated more or less like men, since it was reasoned than an unmarried woman needed the protection of the law, With the exception of the right to vote and sit on a jury, a single Englishwoman enjoyed a good deal of freedom, at least by contemporary standards.

Women on the Continent often fared even worse. The legislation of Napoleon Bonaparte changed the laws of equality which had been in force during the Revolution, leaving women without any legal protection from violent husbands.

The American Experience — The Colonial Period

The men and women who first colonized the United States brought with them religious and social traditions which were clearly patriarchal in nature; most Protestant sects believed that Eve was the first to come under the devil's spell and that Woman was responsible for the world's evil. Calvin and Knox, both influential in Protestant thought, were totally against equality for women, and the Colonies certainly did not escape the witch hunting fervor of the sixteenth and seventeenth centuries.[34] However, the Puritans did teach that although the man retained total authority in the home, husband and wife were expected to live with mutual affection and respect. Furthermore, laws existed which forbade a man to beat his wife or force her to disobey God's law.[35]

Generally speaking, colonial women had considerable status and freedom simply because their talents and labors were needed in the unsettled country. Women ran taverns and rooming houses, and acted as blacksmiths, tailors, teachers, and shopkeepers. They also had a reasonably good chance of owning property; land grants were sometimes given to widows and to the wives of settlers.[36] Because of their important economic position, the law was sometimes "stretched" to allow women to participate in legal proceedings such as suing to collect payments.[37]

Colonial law recognized a wife's right to share her husband's home and bed, be supported by him, and be protected from his violence.[38] However, women were still generally not permitted to sue in court, so many of the rights they possessed in theory were, in practice, basically meaningless. In fact, it was not until the 1880's, with the growth of the women's movement, that there was any serious challenge to "couverture." In short, colonial women were allowed greater flexibility in their roles only as long as these new freedoms did not substantially threaten the patriarchal system.[39]

The American Revolution, while securing more rights and freedoms for men, did little to further the progress of women; there was a noticeable lack of the mention of women in both the Declaration of Independence and in the proposed Constitution. This "oversight" did not go unnoticed by all. Abigail Adams, for example, expressed her disapproval of the new power structure in a letter to her husband in April, 1776. Mr. Adams was not pleased by his wife's opinions and wrote the following in reply: "At your extraordinary code of laws I cannot but laugh. We have been told that our struggle has loosened the bonds of government everywhere—children and apprentices. . .schools and colleges. . .Indians and Negroes grow insolent. But your letter was the first intimation that another tribe more numerous and powerful than the rest, were grown discontented. . . Depend on it, we know better than to repeal our masculine systems."[40]

Post Revolutionary War and the Victorian Period

In the first decades of the 1800's, social and economic changes took place which would have a profound effect on the lives of women for the next 170 years. A new middle class developed which lived in urban areas and earned its living from business. In this middle class, home and family were seen as being separate from the world of work. For the first time, women performed traditional work but earned no money for it. Women, once considered partners, became dependents, entirely supported by their husbands.[41] Furthermore, with growing industrialization, the factory, not the home, soon became the major producer of goods. A woman's reliance upon her husband's earnings was therefore increased, since there was no other way to obtain the needed products. During this period women were also slowly closed off from some of the economic opportunities they had earlier enjoyed. For example, in many trades once practiced by women, formal instruction was newly required. Women were barred from this training.

With regard to legal practices in the United States, the most influential was English Common Law which had been adopted by all the Colonies except Connecticut, and later Louisiana, which adopted the Napoleonic Code. The first United States court to acknowledge a husband's right to correct his wife was in Mississippi. In 1824 the decision in Bradley vs. the State of Mississippi found that a man should be allowed to ". . .moderately chastise his wife without subjecting himself to the vexatious prosecutions for assault and battery, resulting in the discredit and shame of all parties concerned."[42]

The next fifty or sixty years did see some improvement in

statutes related to domestic violence. States such as Maryland, Alabama, and New Hampshire passed laws forbidding wifebeating.[43] However, a woman still could not obtain redress in court because she was a "femme couvert." Furthermore, in North Carolina in 1864, a precedent was established which profoundly influenced the courts' attitude toward wifebeating. In the State vs. Black, it was found that wifebeating was a matter best left out of the courts unless "some permanent injury be inflicted or there be an excess of violence. Otherwise the law will not invade the domestic forum. . . ." The law was to ". . .leave the parties to make the matter up and to live together as man and wife should."[44]

During this period there was also a great deal of discussion about a man's "sphere" and a woman's "sphere." In fact, an entire theory of personality evolved based on the notion that men and women were total opposites in both physical constitution and temperament. In the 1700's differences between male and female were acknowledged, but there was considerable flexibility. For example, it was quite possible, indeed necessary, for a woman of that period to be strong, self-confident, and perhaps even adventurous. By the 1800's, however, this had changed. Women were viewed as being timid, gentle, helpless, and weak.[45]

An excellent example of this new "psychology" is found in Thomas Dew's classic dissertation, "The Differences Between the Sexes": "The greater strength of man, enables him to occupy the foreground in the picture. . .he plunges into the turmoil and bustle of an active, selfish world. . .hence courage and boldness are his attributes. . . He is the shield of woman, destined by nature to guard and protect her. Her inferior strength and sedentary habits confine her within the domestic circle. . .she is not familiarized with the out of door dangers and hardships of a cold and scuffling world; timidity and modesty are her attribute. . .Grace, charm, and loveliness are the charms which constitute her power. By these she creates the magic spell that subdues to her will, the more mighty physical powers by which she is surrounded."[46] In other words, within only fifty years, society had conveniently chosen to forget that colonial women had routinely put in long, arduous hours on farms and in homes, and were therefore quite capable of doing hard work. Moreover, the emphasis on physical strength was a spurious argument because the middle class depended on commerce. A shopkeeper, lawyer, doctor, or businessman needed intellect, not physical prowess, in order to become successful.

Protestant theologians also expressed the view that a woman belonged in the home. For example, in Jonathon Stearns' *Female Influence, and the True Christian Mode of Its Exercise*, he stated, ". . .there is a *natural difference* in the mental as well as the physical constitution of the two classes men and women —a difference which implies not *inferiority* on one part, but only *adaptation to a different sphere*."[47] Stearns went on to say that although some women were certainly capable of public debate, this was not an appropriate activity. It was not a question of ability, but rather a matter of decency and "Christian propriety."

During the Victorian period, motherhood was considered to be the middle class woman's most important job. In fact, the bearing and raising of children became elevated to an almost saintly duty. It was, therefore, all the more important for women to retain their refinement, innocence, and passivity so that they would have the proper effect on their offspring.

Victorian women were also kept confined because of the theory of the law of conservation of energy, which stated that one organ or ability could not be developed without it being at the expense of all others. Since childbearing was supposedly the central reason for a woman's existence, it was thought dangerous to divert any energy away from reproduction. One of the consequences of their theory was that higher education for women was viewed by some as a potential threat to the future of the entire race. As one physician wrote, "If we wish

61

woman to fulfill the task of motherhood fully, she cannot possess a masculine brain. If the feminine abilities were developed to the same degree as those of the male, her maternal organs would suffer and we should have before us a repulsive and useless hybrid."[48]

During the Victorian period, then, women's lives were highly circumscribed. Medical science and psychology taught them that they were far too weak and fragile for anything but their prime duty—child-bearing. Economic and legal factors kept them dependent on their husbands, and religious leaders threatened dire consequences if women dared to venture beyond their appropriate "sphere." However, the practice of keeping women at home, carefully segregated from "outside" activities, carried within it the seeds of its own destruction: "Ideas about women's place in the nineteenth century forced women into very close relationships with one another. When women were together, they talked about their lives. Even as they comforted one another, they also complained, and eventually they grew angry. It was no accident that the nineteenth century women's movement was conceived at a ladies' tea party."[49]

The Suffrage Movement and the Emergence of the Modern Woman (1890 to the late 1960's)

By the end of the nineteenth century women had gained status in several areas. Although there had been no extensive legal reform, by 1890 many states had modified "couverture," giving women control over their inherited property and earnings. Women also found new employment opportunities as typists and stenographers. However, the 1890's also saw the "feminization" of many occupations. "Feminization" is a process in which women become the majority within a profession, leaving only a very small number of men who then take the leadership positions. The prestige of the field is thereby reduced.[50]

Advances for women in education were less equivocal. At the

62

beginning of the nineteenth century no colleges had accepted women. In 1900, by contrast, 80% of all colleges, universities, and professional schools allowed women to enroll. The importance of these opportunities should not be underestimated. Women not only increased their academic knowledge but also gained the self-confidence necessary for them to begin questioning their "proper" place in society.[51]

The 1890's also experienced a growth in the number and type of women's organizations. However, the accomplishments of the suffrage movement were far from impressive. Part of this failure was due to the efforts of a vigorous anti-suffrage campaign, frequently led by socially prominent women. Their argument was quite simple: if women voted they would eventually hold office, and if they held office, they would have to leave home, thereby breaking up families. Therefore, until 1912, the suffrage movement was not very influential.[52]

In the years directly preceding 1920, however, the woman's movement gained strength and purpose. The ranks were joined by new leaders, many of whom had been in England and had observed the tactics used there. Furthermore, the Progressive Party had included woman's suffrage as part of their platform. Between 1910 and 1914, six states gave the vote to women. In August, 1920, with ratification by Tennessee, the Nineteenth Amendment giving women the right to vote became law.[53]

With the passage of this amendment, however, the women's movement seemed to lose its reason for being. The consensus was that women had attained total liberation because suffrage had been won. This attitude led to a backlash, and by the late 1920's there was a new anti-feminism which argued that women simply were not capable of successfully combining marriage and a career.[54] The woman who did work often became disillusioned when she discovered how difficult it was to "juggle" a job and family in a society which was not supportive of those efforts. ". . .the mass of educated married women no longer

63

believed that paid employment was worth the trouble. Why should they exhaust themselves with complicated alternatives to their usual routines when it was easier to stay at home and cultivate that higher domesticity which, it was now understood, had been the real purpose of the woman's movement all along?"[55]

The woman's movement was also dealt a serious blow by Freudian psychology which had become popular and influential during that period. Freud's theory of sexuality stated that anatomical differences resulted in differences in personality, with women coming out the clear losers. "I [Freud] cannot evade the notion. . .that for women the level of what is ethically normal is different from what it is in men. Their superego is never so inexorable, so impersonal, so independent of its emotional origin as we require it to be in men. Character traits which critics of every epoch have brought up against women— that they show less sense of justice than men, that they are less ready to submit to the great exigencies of life, that they are more often influenced in their judgments by feelings of affection or hostility— all of these would be amply accounted for by the modification in the formation of their superego which we have inferred above. We must not allow ourselves to be deflected from such conclusions by the denials of feminists, who are anxious to force us to regard the two sexes as completely equal in position and worth. . ."[56] The net effect of Freud's psychology was that it lent "scientific support" to the belief that women should be confined to domestic activities.

The Depression and Second World War served to reinforce the view that a woman's proper role was as a wife and mother. Economic and political problems and uncertainties made a stable, traditional family life seem very desirable. During the war, of course, women had worked in large numbers, and had been praised for their participation and sacrifice. However, the woman who worked in the post-war years was no longer being patriotic— she was taking a much-needed job away from a returning veteran.

The professional community also tended to advocate a return to domesticity, a position defended by the popular book, *Modern Woman—The Lost Sex*. Written by a psychiatrist and a sociologist, the book attacked the cultural devaluation of homemaking and motherhood, and claimed that women's desires for "masculine" activities and achievements were responsible for the high level of neurosis and dissatisfaction in society. The solution to this problem was the "feminine mother," the only woman who could raise healthy children. "How does the proper mother bring up her children?. . .she accepts her sexuality and enjoys it without parading it. She does not understand when she hears other women speak bitterly of the privileges of men. Men, to her, are useful objects and if, being useful, they extract enjoyment from various of the strange things they are up to it is quite all right with her. She knows, at any rate, that she is dependent on a man. There is no fantasy in her mind about being an 'independent woman,' a contradiction in terms. . .Having children is to her the most natural thing possible. . .If a woman does not have children, she asks ingenuously, what is everything about for her?"[57]

The problems of middle class women in the 1940's, '50's, and early '60's, were given voice in the now classic, *The Feminine Mystique* by Betty Friedan. In it she described quite cogently the image of the ideal woman. "The American housewife—freed by science and labor saving appliances from drudgery, the dangers of childbirth, and the illnesses of her grandmother. She was healthy, beautiful, educated, and concerned only about her husband, her children, and her home. As a housewife and mother, she was respected as a full and equal partner to man in his world. She was free to choose automobiles, clothes, appliances, supermarkets; she had everything that women ever dreamed of."[58] Although it was acceptable for a woman in the 1950's to work outside the home, a more traditional role was clearly preferable. For example, in 1956 the October 16th issue of *Look* magazine stated, "The American woman is winning the battle of the sexes. Like a teen-

65

ager, she is growing up and confounding her critics. . . No longer a psychological immigrant to man's world, she works, rather casually, as a third of the U.S. labor force, less towards a "big career" than as a way of filling a hope chest or buying a new home freezer. She gracefully concedes the top jobs to men. This wondrous creature also marries younger than ever, has more babies and looks and acts far more feminine than the 'emacipated girl' of the 1920's and 1930's. Steel worker's wife and junior leaguer alike do their own housework. . . .Today if she makes an old fashioned choice, and lovingly tends a garden and a bumper crop of children, she rates louder hosannahs than ever before."

But if American society were loud in praise of the "traditional woman," it had scorn and criticism for those who dared venture outside of that role. The bright, well educated, and ambitious career woman was characterized as being so frustrated and masculinized by her career that her husband became indifferent to her sexually and usually drowned his problems in alcoholism. But it wasn't enough to be a housewife and mother in terms of behavior alone; the ideal woman's whole psychological, emotional and spiritual life was to be immersed in those activities. The Christmas 1956 issue of *Life* magazine warned of the dangers of the woman who had either worked before marriage or was well educated and then found herself discontented with being "just a housewife." The article asserted that such dissatisfaction could damage the lives of herself and her family as much as if she were a career woman.

Therefore, in the period from the late 1940's until the late sixties, the only socially acceptable role for a woman was as a wife and mother. As mentioned earlier, such a restrictive attitude indirectly perpetuates battering situations. The woman who is too emotionally and financially dependent on her husband may find it difficult, if not impossible, to survive on her own.

CHAPTER III

SOCIAL FACTORS CURRENTLY CONTRIBUTING TO
THE INCIDENCE OF WIFE ABUSE

Because of the vigor and scope of the women's movement in the last few years, one might conclue that many of the factors which once contributed to the incidence of wifebeating are no longer present. However, there are still elements of our society which perpetuate the physical abuse of women.

Social Sanction

We as a society still give informal sanction to domestic violence. For example, only nine years ago an attitude survey found that one fifth of all Americans approved of slapping one's spouse on "appropriate occasions." Contrary to the myth that wifebeating is a lower-class phenomenon, this study showed that the higher the respondent's education and income level, the more likely he or she was to approve of physical aggression between husband and wife.[1] In addition, consider the results of a field study in which assaults were staged on a street corner. Male witnesses came to the aid of men being assaulted by other men, helped women being assaulted by other women, and even interceded for men being attacked by women. However, not one male bystander intervened to help when a woman was assaulted by a man.[2]

Violence in the Media
It is apparent that depicting the physical abuse of women is quite lucrative; record album covers, billboards, and advertisements picture women bound, gagged, whipped, chained, and as victims of murder, sexual assault, and gang rape. However degrading, these images apparently sell well. For example, the Atlantic/Avco Records magazine copy of The Rolling Stones' album, "Black and Blue" pictures a woman who has obviously been beaten. Although this woman is still tied up, she appears seductive, as if asking for more abuse. In reality, of course, a bruised and battered woman's face is hardly appealing. However, the photo gives the impression that no real damage has been done. Both billboard and the magazine article state, "I'm black and blue from the Rolling Stones, and I love it." This graphic was used in at least five major industry consumer magazines for a period of two months.[3]

But apparently the advertising business is not alone in finding it profitable to portray the abuse of women. In the past few years Hollywood has produced a number of horror movies which feature graphic scenes of violence against women. Of course, there is nothing new about horror films per se; moviegoers have always been willing to pay the price of admission in order to be frightened and shocked by what they knew would appear on the screen. However, according to Gene Siskel, film critic for the Chicago Tribune, the new movies are significantly different from past horror classics.

To begin with, in earlier films the antagonists were figures drawn from our nightmares and fantasies. When beautiful women were in peril, they were menaced by Dracula, the Mummy, or a Creature from the Black Lagoon. By contrast, today's monsters are very human —emotionally disturbed men who, unable to relate to the opposite sex, take out their anger and frustration by brutalizing women.

In addition, in current films extraordinary attention is given to the attacks on the heroine. Formerly, a director might use one or two shots of the struggle, letting most of the violence take place off camera. However, in contemporary movies such as "I Spit on Your Grave" and "The Last House on the Left," acts of rape, torture, and murder are shown in graphic, repetitious detail. Furthermore, it cannot be argued that these scenes are added for the sake of artistry. It is quite possible to elicit feelings of terror without resorting to such devices. Instead, excessive violence is used for the simple reason that people want to see it and will pay to see it.

The new genre of films also departs from tradition in terms of perspective. In the past, the story was typically seen through the eyes of the victim or victims, making it easy for the audience to identify with them in their fight against evil. Now, it is common for action to be depicted from the standpoint of the attacker. This encourages viewers to identify with the assailant, giving them the opportunity to vicariously experience the act of raping and/or murdering a woman.

Finally, the new horror movies contain a disturbing subliminal message— women who are independent or get "out of line" pay for it by being assaulted. The victims of today's monsters are women who go on vacation alone, work late in a deserted office, or assert themselves in some way. These recent "shock" films have been quite successful financially, primarily because of their ability to attract large numbers of teenagers. Considering the content of these films, the implications for the future are chilling.

Myths and Stereotypes

Current myths and stereotypes about wife abuse tend to make the victim feel ashamed and reluctant to seek help, and also cause others to view her as undeserving of aid. As mentioned earlier, there is a tendency to believe that the battered woman stays because she "likes it." Therefore, people often see little reason to help a person who purposefully chooses to be mistreated. The battered woman herself may also come to believe this myth. Regardless of how she truly feels, she may begin to suspect that perhaps she really is a masochist. This increases her shame and makes it even less likely that she will tell anyone about the problem.

Economics

Present economic conditions often make it very difficult for a woman to escape from a violent situation. Women are still primarily in a small number of low paying occupations, with relatively few being found in professional and technical fields. In addition, one study of income levels found that a woman made an average of $3458 less than a man in a comparable position. By 1973, this figure had improved by only one percent.[4] In addition, women who become divorced frequently experience economic deprivation and cannot even always depend on alimony; the majority of men do not contribute to the support of their wives and children after the separation.[5]

Legal Aspects

Although there are no longer laws which give a man the right to beat his wife, it is still very difficult for a battered woman to take legal action against her husband. At each stage in the process of criminal or civil prosecution, a woman may encounter problems substantial enough to discourage her from proceeding any further. The following is a list of the events in a typical wifebeating case:

1. A complaint is made—
    The moment the police are called, decisions are made which have considerable impact on the case. To

70

begin with, the dispatcher may not immediately send a unit to the scene. This is because wife abuse is frequently viewed as a "family problem," not a crime like burglary or assault. In general, society still believes that a man's home is his castle and that the state's intervention must be viewed with considerable caution. In addition, officers themselves are often reluctant to respond to a family disturbance—and with good reason. FBI statistics indicate that one quarter of the police officers who are killed or injured on duty receive these injuries while responding to domestic disturbance calls. Although in some instances, police officers do respond quite quickly, women have had to wait up to an hour for a unit to arrive. By that time, potential witnesses and the man himself may have left the scene, making an arrest or even a thorough investigation virtually impossible.

2. **An officer responds—**

At this point a woman may encounter problems related to the officer's own perception of "the battered woman." Unless he has had special training, he is likely to have formed a stereotyped image. Many police have had the experience of being called to the same house every weekend. The officer may even be on a first name basis with the couple. In these "Saturday night scuffles," the scenario is almost always the same: the police arrive, get the man to leave for awhile, and the woman never wants her husband arrested. If an officer has had no other contact with wifebeating cases, it may be difficult for a woman to convince him that she is serious about pressing charges. Some women have even reported that a police officer tried to discourage them from having their hus-

71

bands arrested.

Another—and often unspoken—problem is that the police officer himself may be violent at home. Karen Bustos, a Deputy District Attorney in San Bernardino County, describes the situation this way: "It's a very "macho" kind of thing, because you're talking about a man in the middle of the twentieth century with a gun on his hip. It's not 1850 in Dodge City where all the men carried guns and everybody had a shotgun over the hearth to either shoot the Indians or shoot the dinner. There is an authoritarian personality, I think, in some police officers. It has to do with power, and there is no reason to believe that the violence between a police officer and his wife is any less than what you'd find in the general population. In fact, I would not be surprised if it were more."

This is also the point at which it is important for officers to collect physical evidence, interview witnesses, and make observations that would be important in a subsequent trial. Unfortunately, detailed evidence gathering is rare, because officers know that there is a good chance the case will never be filed. For reasons that will be discussed later, many women change their minds about prosecuting the case. Again quoting Karen Bustos, "When an officer goes to the scene of a homicide, it's, 'Call the pathologist, call the coroner, call the detectives, call the identification bureau, get the helicopter out here, roll *everyone*, because this is a capital case.' But a 'family 415,' (California Penal Code section for disturbing the peace) is: 'Lots of work, and she may love him next week and won't prosecute, and I'm going to do a lot of work for nothing, and it's very frustrating'." Therefore, unless an officer has reason to believe that a woman is serious about pressing charges, he may not do a thorough investigation.

Still another problem is that the very act of obtaining evidence can be distressing. A woman's injuries must be documented, and one of the best methods is to have photographs which can later be shown to a jury. However, going to a police station and having pictures taken of one's nude body is a traumatic experience in itself. But without such procedures, the district attorney would not be able to file charges for lack of evidence. Many women are unaware of the need for such kinds of information, and even if they are later willing to press charges, they often cannot because of an inadequate investigation.

3.   An arrest is made—

Even if a man is taken into custody, a woman still finds herself in danger. To begin with, her husband is eligible to post bail, and may be released within hours. Since he is likely to be very angry, she may well be beaten again when he returns home. Furthermore, if she presses charges, a trial will not be held for several months. Therefore, she must either get a restraining order—which, because it is not easily enforceable, does not guarantee her safety—or she and her children must have another place to live. For a woman with limited financial means, the latter solution is sometimes impossible, and moving in with friends or family increases the possibility that her husband will find her.

4.   Awaiting trial—

The period between the arrest and the trial can be

very difficult. The woman may begin to feel sorry for her husband and not want him to lose his job, have a record, or go to jail. The unemployed husband also presents a very real threat to a woman who is dependent upon her spouse for support. Other family members may also pressure her to drop the charges. She is admonished against "airing the dirty linen in public," and she is told that what she is doing to her husband is far out of proportion to his supposed misbehavior. Most battered women, I think, are not really eager to have their husbands put in jail. What they would like is to have their spouses stop being violent so that a good relationship can be developed. Given these circumstances, it is not surprising that many cases never reach trial.

5. **The trial—**

The trial itself can be traumatic. The woman must discuss the most intimate aspects of her life in front of twelve strangers and assembled public and press. Furthermore, anything about the woman is usually considered "fair game," and, as in the case of rape, the defense may make every effort to show that the woman indeed provoked her husband. The defense may also try to cast aspersions on her morality and fitness as a mother, although these factors do not bear directly upon the case. A wifebeating trial is emotionally draining. Invariably, all the hostility and emotional undercurrents in the relationship come out into the open, either directly or through innuendo.

6. **Sentencing—**

Unfortunately, after all the time and trouble of

criminal proceedings, the net effect may be that the problem of violence has not been solved. If a man is found guilty and sent to prison, for example, it is highly unlikely that he will receive rehabilitation which will help him deal with his attitudes towards women and with his uncontrollable anger. Therefore, one can reasonably assume that he will go into prison a batterer, and come out of prison a batterer. Furthermore, the threat of a jail sentence is probably no more of a deterrent to wife-beating than it is to any other crime. If the man is put on probation, sometimes this can be of value, if family counseling is ordered by the court. Of course, unless a man is genuinely motivated to deal with his problem, a court order will not make him change. Many therapists have found that batterers can be quite manipulative and may attend family counseling but not really participate in the therapy.

Civil proceedings can be equally frustrating. It is generally agreed that a restraining order is difficult to enforce and cannot provide guaranteed protection. In many cases, men repeatedly violate restraining orders with relative impunity, particularly if the penalty for violation is only contempt of court. In fact, recently there was a case of a woman whose husband twice violated the restraining order against him. Eventually he broke into the house and murdered his wife. Even divorce does not always ensure a woman's peace of mind and personal safety. Many battered women are harrassed and even attacked by their ex-husbands. Furthermore, there is a tendency for those in the criminal justice system to view the situation as if the couple were still married. Although the woman does have the advantage of

75

having demonstrated that she does not want to remain married, it is still often difficult for her to get any legal satisfaction.

In short, then, although a woman is theoretically protected by law from the violence of her husband, in practice her alternatives are quite limited.

Religion

Certainly, religious views regarding domestic violence have changed. It would be rare, if not unheard of, to find a pastor or priest who advocated wifebeating. However, many denominations still expect members to adhere to traditional roles, and also view divorce as unacceptable. Such attitudes make it very difficult for a woman to end even a violent relationship. Furthermore, many battered women have had the experience of being told by a priest or pastor that they should be good Christians and forgive their husbands. In fact, a number of women have called hotlines asking for reassurance that they were not committing a sin by dissolving a marriage in which they and sometimes the children were being beaten.

Sex-Role Models

It cannot be denied that societal definitions of "masculinity" and "femininity" have become more flexible. However, more traditional sex role models still exist. For example, only a few years ago a popular book, *How to Get and Hold a Woman*, written by a marriage counselor, gave men the following advice: "Why ask women when they only need to be told? Why ask women when they hope to be taken? . . .feelings, moods, and attitudes rule a woman, not facts, reason or logic. . . The acquisition of knowledge or responsibility does not lessen women's need for support, guidance, and control. Quite the contrary."[6]

But now a woman need not content herself by merely reading about her proper role in life — she can even take classes which will teach her how to be feminine and appealing to men. The popularity of these classes should not be underestimated; literally thousands of women have enrolled in "Total Womanhood" and "Fascinating Womanhood" courses. The prospective "total woman" is at least given some good advice—she is told to understand, accept, love, and above all, *be* herself. However, the cornerstone of this philosophy is that a wife must, at all times and in all things, adapt to her husband. "It is only when a woman surrenders her life to her husband, reveres and worships him, and is willing to serve him, that she becomes really beautiful to him. She becomes a priceless jewel, the glory of feminity, his queen."[7]

The woman who enrolls in a "Fascinating Womanhood" course learns that if she wants to be feminine she must accentuate the differences between male and female, and lack—or appear to lack—masculine aggressiveness, competency, efficiency, and fearlessness. It is also emphasized that a wife is expected to be submissive and yield to her husband's rule in all matters. In fact, she is expected to be completely dependent upon her spouse. "Women were designed to be wives, mothers, and homemakers and are, therefore, in need of masculine help to make their way through life. The men were assigned to fill this need for women by serving as their guide, protector, and provider."[8] In the philosophies of both "total" and "fascinating" womanhood, women are valued not for themselves, but for the "support services" they provide for the *really* important people—husbands and children. It is also worth noting that God and the Bible are cited as the final authority for the delineation of male and female roles. Now, if all this sounds familiar to you, you're right; these philosophies are almost identical to those expressed over one hundred years ago.

Although there are no male counterparts to these classes for women, society still generally expects men to adhere to a traditional role. For instance, the socialization of boys is more intense than that of girls; boys are more frequently praised and punished and also receive more pressure to avoid behaving in a sex-inappropriate manner.[9] The need to avoid anything feminine can result in "compulsive masculinity." "When he (a boy) sees women as weak, easily damaged, lacking strength in mind and body, able to perform only tasks which take the least strength and are of least importance, what boy in his right senses would not give his all to escape this alternative to the male role? For many, unfortunately, the scramble to escape takes on all the aspects of panic, and the outward semblance of non-feminity is achieved at a tremendous cost of anxiety and self-alienation."[10]

Adherence to a rigid masculine role can be both physically and psychologically damaging. Men are expected to achieve, to get ahead, and to stay "cool." However, winning once is not enough—to be a "real" man, one has to keep winning. Not surprisingly, the need to stay ahead produces considerable stress,[11] which may be responsible, in part, for the fact that males have a higher risk of heart attack and tend to die earlier than do females.[12] In addition, men tend to be low in self-disclosure. This may make it quite difficult for them to relate to women since a person who is afraid to reveal himself is likely to feel threatened by intimacy.[13] Society also teaches that ". . .'real men' are never passive or dependent, always dominant in relationships with women or other men, and don't talk about or directly express feelings; especially feelings that don't contribute to dominance."[14] Finally, men have usually learned to ignore both physical symptoms and emotions until they become too strong to escape notice. It is possible that batterers do not become aware of their own feelings of anger or frustration until the pressure in unbearable. These men then overreact with aggression. The violence would not only allow for an acceptable "male" display of emotion, but also re-establish his superiority.

It is not just the general public that supports traditional models of behavior. Many professionals—ministers, psychiatrists, lawyers—accept these stereotypes as well. For example, some psychologists and psychiatrists still believe that women are by nature masochistic. The "traditional" explanation for wife abuse is that women seek out violent men and remain in the relationship simply because they enjoy suffering.[15] A number of battered wives have related "horror stories" about their contact with counselors. One woman described her experience this way: "My therapist told me I could keep my husband from being violent by acting more feminine. You may find this hard to believe but he actually said that when I was sitting across from my husband, I should slump down in my chair so I wouldn't appear so tall, strong and independent. He also suggested that I speak more quietly and stop trying to run things. Needless to say, none of that did any good. Eventually I found myself another therapist—and another husband." Fortunately, this woman realized that she had been given very poor advice. Unfortunately, many women take similar instructions in good faith and suffer.

Even therapists who do not adhere to sexual stereotypes often find it difficult to provide adequate counseling for violent couples. Relatively few counselors have had extensive experience dealing with this problem, and are therefore unacquainted with the psychodynamics and social factors which are involved. It is particularly devastating to a battered woman to have contact with a professional who is not well trained. It is one thing for a friend to tell her that the beatings are her fault and that perhaps she really does enjoy the abuse. It is quite another when an authority figure or "expert" draws the same conclusion.

CHAPTER IV

WHO IS THE BATTERED WOMAN?

It is fair to say that almost any woman could be hit, or even beaten once. However, most battered women share certain personality traits which increase the likelihood of their becoming "trapped" in a violent relationship.

Low Self-Esteem

At present, there does not appear to be any one factor which is common to the backgrounds of all battered women. Nevertheless, whatever their childhood experiences, it is apparent that they do not grow up with feelings of high self-esteem. This perceived lack of self worth is reflected in their selection of a marriage partner; battered women consistently "marry down" by choosing men who come from lower socio-economic groups than they. Later on, this lack of self-worth may make her particularly vulnerable to her husband's verbal attacks. As the emotional abuse increases, it will be hard for her not to believe her husband when he tells her that she is worthless and incompetent. Eventually, she may conclude that she simply does not deserve anything better and, therefore, may give up her attempts to improve the situation or to get out.

Adherence to traditional sex-role models

Most battered women try to fulfill traditional, stereotyped images of femininity. In short, they tend to see themselves primarily as wives and mothers rather than as individuals, and believe that they should be nurturant, submissive, and forgiving of their spouses' frailties. Brought up to be dependent upon their husbands, these women are likely to feel quite threatened by the prospect of being on their own. Furthermore, "traditional" wives tend to view the relative success of their marriages as a reflection of their worth as human beings. Therefore, they may see divorce as a threat in terms of economics and social stigma, as well as evidence of personal failure.

Inability to deal with anger

Battered women usually find it difficult to deal directly and appropriately with feelings of anger. Some women become violent themselves, venting their aggression upon their spouses or children. However, many abused women grew up believing that it was unacceptable to express anger, and thus direct their hostility inward. This, in turn, may result in depression. Although these depressions are often transient, they can be long-term and debilitating. For example, one woman reported that for eight months it was all she could do just to get her child off to school in the morning. Then she simply sat in a chair and stared blankly at the television or a wall until late afternoon. Of course, many wives do find ways of passively aggressing. For example, they may "get back at" their mates by serving unappetizing foods, by not doing the laundry, or by "forgetting" to awaken their husbands in time for an important appointment.

Lack of self-nurturance

The battered woman has a tendency to put everyone else's

81

needs before her own. It is not uncommon for a wife to be beaten for several years, leaving only when her husband begins to abuse the children. In other words, these women do not feel that they themselves deserve a non-violent relationship, but refuse to let their children be hurt. When women do get into shelters and participate in group therapy, it is sometimes difficult to get them to talk about their own feelings, needs and desires. Instead, they frequently focus their conversation on husbands, family or children. It often takes many sessions before a battered wife allows herself to think in terms of what *she* wants to do with her life.

CHAPTER V

WHAT KIND OF MAN BEATS A WOMAN?

Because domestic violence is so widespread, it is unlikely that there is one "personality type" which is characteristic of all violent men. Nevertheless, it is still possible to identify some common factors:

Family Background

Approximately half of the men who batter their wives were abused themselves as children or saw their own mothers being beaten. It is also typical to find that there had been alcoholism, neglect, or an unhealthy relationship with one or both parents. For example, many batterers were, as children, very attached to indulgent and overprotective mothers. This maternal dependency often continues well beyond childhood; it is not unusual for these men to turn to their mothers rather than to their wives for emotional support. Many battered women found that their mothers-in-law had an unreasonable degree of influence over their sons and had a tendency to interfere in the marriage. Paternal relationships do not appear to have been much better. In many cases sons were either neglected by their fathers or were engaged in an intense competition which frequently continued into adulthood. In short, one rarely—if ever— finds that a violent man came from a happy, well-adjusted family.

83

Personality Characteristics
Insecurity—
Whatever their childhood experiences, batterers grow up feeling very insecure as adults. This insecurity is usually reflected in extreme jealousy. The jealousy is usually sexual in nature, and men rarely confine their suspicions to any one particular person. Instead, women are usually accused of taking many lovers, from company executives to the paperboy. Sometimes, violent men become quite paranoid about their wives' supposed infidelity. It is not uncommon for a husband to put a "tap" on the phone, or to have someone follow his spouse. One man actually timed how long it took his wife to get to the laundry room from their apartment, telephoning her to make sure she didn't "meet her boyfriend" in between.

Poor Verbal Communication—
Violent men tend to have difficulty verbally expressing their emotions. Although they may communicate well in professional life, they are often unable to tell their wives about feelings and personal needs. Such a man expects his mate to know what he wants without his having to say anything. When she is unable to do so, he may interpret this as meaning she does not really love him, and react to this "rejection" with violence. A wife-beater is rarely capable of true intimacy and may, in fact, feel very threatened by the prospect of being "open" and vulnerable.

Dominating—
Most batterers are quite dominating, demanding control over almost every aspect of their marriages; they expect to make all major decisions, and frequently become angry if their wives disagree or act independently. Almost without exception, these

84

men feel they have the right to monitor their wives' activities outside the home. Some husbands try to restrict their mates by refusing to let them go back to school, or even to church. Other men actually insist upon choosing their wives' friends for them. The net effect is that the battered woman usually becomes socially isolated, and is, therefore, totally dependent on her husband for emotional support, such as it is. In addition, it is relatively easy for him to influence or even determine her attitudes about herself and the marriage. In many cases, a batterer may convince his spouse that she is a bad wife and mother who is entirely deserving of the beatings she receives.

"Dual Personality"—

Although the vast majority of violent men are not psychotic, they can sometimes almost appear to be two different people. Some, but not all, batterers are capable of being very friendly and charming to people outside the family. In public, such a man may be so nice, and so easy going, that if his wife does tell someone about the beatings, she will probably be met with disbelief. In extreme cases, these men have been described as "con artists" who sometimes are able to convince police officers, lawyers, and judges that their wives' accounts of violence should not be taken seriously.

Lack of Assertiveness—

At first, it might appear that the problem with violent men is that they are *too* assertive. However, many batterers who are "tyrants" in their own homes may be quite passive in other situations. Furthermore, the truly assertive person is not aggressive. Instead, he stands up for his rights without running "roughshod" over the rights of others. By contrast, the batterer may not speak up when he feels exploited, keeping his anger and frustration "bottled up" inside until he gets home. Then he may overreact with violence to the slightest threat to his status.

Adherence to Traditional Sex-Role Model—

The man who beats his wife tends to adhere to a stereo-typed model of masculine behavior, a role which requires that he: (1) never appears weak; (2) can solve his problems without asking for help; (3) make all important family decisions; (4) receive deferential treatment from his wife and children; and (5) be in control of his emotions, especially in public. The batterer typically expects his wife to fulfill a traditional sex role as well. He expects her to be responsible for all household and "mothering" chores and to be submissive and subservient. Because the wifebeater is already insecure, the most innocuous of actions may be perceived as a threat to his "masculine superiority." For example, a man might hit his wife because she served the children's dinner plates before his.

Dependency Needs—

Many battered women have found that when they actually left their husbands and filed for divorce their spouses made extraordinary attempts to persuade them to return. It is not unusual for a women to find herself beseiged by phone calls, letters, unwanted gifts, and unwanted visits from her husband. He may claim that he loves her, cannot live without her, and will do anything she wants if only she will come back. Some men even threaten to commit suicide, although only a very few do kill themselves.

It has been suggested that men become violent because of a conflict between their dependency needs and their desire to be "masculine" and dominant. Although this may be true in

86

some cases, my research revealed that men who were relatively more dependent on their wives were actually less severe in their violence. They also displayed less hostility toward their mates than did men who were more independent. Such behavior makes good intuitive sense; if a man is very dependent on his wife it is less likely that he will want to risk having his spouse leave him.

Contradictory 'Traits—

All human behavior is complex, but batterers in particular often seem to display contradictory behavior. For example, some men severely beat their wives and yet never physically harm the children. In one case, for example, a man had had a record of juvenile arrests because of violence, had been a boxer in the army, and was extremely abusive toward his wife. Yet this same man was a professional gardener who carefully nurtured beautiful flowers and patiently encouraged his sons in their own gardening efforts. And, although he would almost never sit down and talk to his wife, when he was out of town he would write her eloquent love letters.

Although family background and personality traits are certainly important factors in domestic violence, we must also consider two other reasons that men continue to beat their wives. First, it is often very difficult for batterers to get help. Only a few therapists have had much experience in dealing with this problem. Second, in most cases, a man can get what he wants from beating his mate (the restoration of his dominance, a feeling of being "one up" on someone, release of built up tension, etc.) without fear of being punished for his actions.

CHAPTER VI

PATTERNS OF INTERACTION AMONG VIOLENT COUPLES

Pre-Battering Stage

This phase begins when the couple first meets and can last a few days or for several years. During this period, some men are violent to inanimate objects. When they get angry they may throw or break lamps, chairs, dishes, or tables. In some cases, a man may even take out his hostility on family pets. Although a husband may be verbally abusive to his wife, this "emotional battering" is usually not as intensive or malicious as in later stages.

The First Incident

Although the initial act of violence is sometimes quite severe, it is ordinarily relatively "minor"; men slap their wives, shove them, or push them up against a wall. The first beating usually takes place during an argument, and/or at a time when the couple is experiencing external stress such as the loss of a job, the birth of a child, or a death in the family. Both the man and the woman tend to minimize the importance of this incident. For instance, if they have been arguing, a man may rationalize his behavior by saying that his wife became hysterical and that he hit her to "bring her to her senses." The woman may try to convince herself that the violence was completely out of character for her husband and would, therefore, never happen again. Unfortunately, once a beating has occurred, there will probably be further battering. Apparently, the first incident has the effect of "breaking the ice." Many women have said that, in retrospect, once their husbands discovered they could get away with being violent, it seemed to lower their inhibitions against future and more severe abuse.

Cycles of Violence

In some cases, domestic violence occurs in a cycle comprised of these stages: tension-building, acute battering incident, and "reconciliation." During the last phase, the man is remorseful and tries to be particularly nice to his wife. She forgives him, and the cycles begins anew. It has been suggested that the husband's good behavior is the "reward" which keeps his wife from leaving.[1] On the other hand, it is also quite possible that some women take on the role of "rescuer." The very act of "rescuing"—forgiving the partner and protecting him from the consequences of his behavior by keeping his violence a secret—fosters dependency in the man and confers power upon the woman. For a short period of time, at least, she enjoys superiority over the husband.

Progressive Deterioration

The cycle described above, however, is not universal. Instead, many couples experience a consistent worsening of their relationship. The initial incident of battering introduces elements of stress and mistrust into the marriage. Despite the man's promises that it will never happen again, the possibility for future violence is always there. Because of this, the quality of their interaction never returns to the level it was before the first beating. Other important changes also occur. To begin with, there is a sharp reduction in the amount of verbal communication between the man and woman. In fact, some couples never even talk about the violence. As one woman said, "My husband would beat me up one night, give me no more than an 'I'm sorry, but you made me do it,' and the next morning expect me to act as if nothing had happened." Although there may still be many arguments, the couple rarely has productive discussions or shares their feelings with one another. For the woman, this emotional withdrawal may be her only psychological defense against the verbal abuse.

The onset of violence also ordinarily signals a deterioration in the sexual relationship. Many women report that their sexual desires were "the first thing to go." The battered wife frequently finds it difficult to become sexually aroused and may even be repulsed by her spouse's advances.

Characteristics of the Violence

Regardless of whether or not the battering occurs in cycles, there is a tendency for violence to increase in frequency and/or severity over time. The speed with which this increase occurs varies tremendously. In some instances, it may be several years before the effects of the beatings escalate from cuts and bruises to broken bones. In other cases, however, the violence may greatly intensify in a relatively short period. One woman I interviewed had been hospitalized with fractures of her arm, nose, and tailbone after only five months of marriage.

CHAPTER VII

QUESTIONS AND ANSWERS
ABOUT DOMESTIC VIOLENCE

1. **IS IT POSSIBLE TO PREDICT WHETHER OR NOT A MAN WILL BECOME A BATTERER?**

Yes and no. There are no hard and fast rules, but there are some warning signs. The following factors have been associated with violent men:

- Extreme jealousy and/or possessiveness — Unfortunately, many women believe that jealousy is a sign that their husbands or boyfriends care about them. However, jealousy is not really a healthy emotion—it reflects a basic insecurity about oneself and the relationship. Violent men tend to be particularly uncertain about their masculinity, reacting to perceived threats by becoming extremely possessive, controlling and dominating.

- Heavy use of alcohol — Drinking and battering are frequently associated but most experts agree that alcohol itself does not actually cause the violence. Instead, being drunk is used as an excuse. Since society allows a person to disavow his behavior while drinking, a man can claim that he simply didn't know what he was doing, and that he shouldn't be responsible for what happened. His wife may tell herself that he really is a good man, and that alcohol, not her husband, is the problem. Unfortunately, even if a man does stop drinking, it does not necessarily mean that the violence will end.

- The presence of violence in the family background — Approximately one half of the men who batter their wives were either abused themselves as children or watched their own mothers being beaten. Such experiences provide strong role models and this kind of learned behavior is often very difficult to change. Even men who grew up hating their fathers for beating their mothers may eventually abuse their own wives. The cycle of violence is, therefore, likely to continue unless the batterer gets counseling.

- A history of being violent to others — A man who has a reputation for getting into fist fights probably believes that violence is acceptable behavior, and may feel no contrition whatsoever about abusing his spouse. If such a man is criticized for being a wifebeater, he is likely to respond, "Why can't I beat her; she's my wife, isn't she?"

- A compulsive need to be masculine or "macho" — The man who consistently tries to project a "macho" image must always maintain dominance over his wife, must not show his emotions (except anger), and is not supposed to need help. Such a man is likely to use violence as a means of "keeping his wife in line."

2. **MY HUSBAND/BOYFRIEND HAS SLAPPED ME ONCE OR TWICE. SHOULD I BE CONCERNED?**

Yes. It is my personal belief that there is no place in a relationship for *any* violence. Furthermore, once violence has occurred, there is a tendency for it to increase in severity and/or frequency. Many severe cases of battering start out with a slap or a shove. In wife abuse, there is no such thing as a "minor incident." Any act of violence should be taken seriously. It is important that you discuss the incident with your husband or boyfriend. Since it is easier to deal with violence in its early stages, it would be a good idea to seek counseling. Even if you were not badly injured, you should not just "forgive and forget." If you ignore the abuse, you give your unspoken approval to violence and increase the chance of its happening again.

3. **A FRIEND OF MINE HAS JUST TOLD ME THAT SHE IS BEING ABUSED. WHAT CAN I DO TO HELP?**

- Listen to your friend. Try to be supportive and non-judgmental. You can help a great deal just by letting her know you care.

- Do not try to be a psychologist or crisis counselor. Effective therapy requires the presence of an objective third party, who is trained to handle problems without becoming too emotionally involved. Attempting to take on such a responsibility places too much of a burden on you, and denies your friend the professional help she needs. You could suggest that she find a counselor to talk to. A list of community resources can usually be found by calling the Department of Mental Health or your city's Human Resources Department. If you are fortunate enough to have a shelter or hotline for battered women in your area, urge her to take advantage of these services.

- Do not try to "come to the rescue" by solving all your friend's problems for her. Her husband may already have so much control over her life that she has lost confidence in her own ability to make important decisions. If you are too directive, you may only reinforce doubts about her competence.

- You should not attempt to reason with her husband or boyfriend. If he discovers that she has talked with you about the abuse it may only serve to enrage him. Furthermore, it is unlikely that your intervention will be effective; batterers need professional counseling to successfully deal with their violence.

- Don't be surprised if you feel overwhelmed by your friend's troubles. Domestic violence is a complex problem, and there are no simple solutions. Although the situation may not immediately resolve itself, you can still be assured that your understanding and concern are of considerable help. You could offer a copy of this book.

4.   WHY DO SO MANY CASES OF WIFE ABUSE GO UNREPORTED?

You might expect that if a woman had been beaten, she

94

would not hesitate to seek help from law enforcement or a social service agency. However, there are several reasons why wife abuse often remains a hidden crime. To begin with, in many homes it is considered "normal" to have some level of violence between husband and wife. This is most likely to be the case when one or both partners was exposed to violence as a child. A woman who saw her own mother being beaten may grow up believing that all men batter their wives. If she sees her abuse as "just the way things are," it probably won't occur to her that she can take steps to end the violence.

A woman may also be unwilling to report the abuse because she fears reprisal by her husband. It is not unusual for a man to beat his wife even more severely if she calls the police or tells someone else about the abuse. Furthermore, as mentioned earlier, police intervention rarely provides a woman with any real, immediate protection. Therefore, many women come to the conclusion that calling the police is ineffective and that it will only increase the chance of getting an even worse beating.

Another factor in under-reporting is that the majority of battered women blame themselves for the violence and thus feel too guilty, ashamed, and embarrassed to tell anyone about the problem. Rather than face the anticipated disapproval and disgrace, they remain silent, hoping to avoid further battering by trying harder to please their husbands.

Finally, many battered women are married to men who hold positions of high standing in the community. Such a woman may feel she must keep the violence a secret in order to protect her husband's reputation.

5. IF A MAN BEATS HIS WIFE, DOES THAT MEAN HE WILL ALSO ABUSE THE CHILDREN?

It is hard to say. It is quite possible that a man may batter his wife severely, and yet never harm the children. However, wife abuse and child abuse do frequently occur together. Apparently, some men turn on the children just to "get at" their wives. If a woman somehow manages to "keep her cool" despite the beatings, her husband may begin battering the children, knowing full well that *that* will get a reaction out of his wife. In this way he is able to maintain emotional control over her. This tactic often backfires, however. Many women say that they decided to leave because they would not let their children be hurt. Of course, it is not always the man who is the abuser. Since women cannot attack the real object of their anger, they may take out their feelings of frustration and despair on the children.

Even if youngsters are not physically abused, they still suffer emotional trauma. Young children often have trouble sleeping, and wake up in the middle of the night, screaming. They also develop psychosomatic disorders, such as asthma. Some children become so upset that they often throw up after eating and begin to lose weight. As they become older, boys tend to be extremely hostile and aggressive, while girls often regress, withdrawing into their own fantasy worlds.

But perhaps one of the most distressing effects of growing up with violence is that girls may come to believe that all men are abusive, and boys may believe that men have a right to batter their wives. In fact, one woman told me that she finally decided to leave her husband when she came upon their eight-year-old son beating his younger sister. "It really made me angry to see that. I grabbed him and demanded to know what

96

he thought he was doing. He looked me straight in the eye and said, 'If Dad can do it, so can I.'"

6. IF DOMESTIC VIOLENCE IS SO WIDESPREAD, WHY ARE THERE SO FEW SERVICES AVAILABLE TO BATTERED WOMEN?

One of the biggest problems is that we are reluctant to admit that domestic violence even exists. The first study of wife abuse did not appear until 1972. This "selective inattention" has occurred for several reasons. First, it has often been said that the family is the cornerstone of our society, and Americans would all like to think that most homes provide safe, secure environments where children grow up loved and happy. Publicity about the extent of violence necessarily challenges this cherished belief. Second, as mentioned earlier, society still gives tacit approval to wife abuse. This makes it more difficult to gain community support. In addition, wifebeating has been so well hidden that it has been relatively easy for us to convince ourselves that it is not a major problem. Third, many people still believe that the battered woman enjoys the abuse and is, therefore, undeserving of any aid. Finally, domestic violence projects have special requirements. To be truly effective, a program must provide protective shelter for women and their children; it is almost impossible for therapy to be effective when the client must still live in an atmosphere of tension and fear. Such projects are relatively expensive and many communities either lack the necessary resources or are simply not aware enough about the problem to raise the funds.

7. WHY IS IT THAT SO MANY BATTERED WOMEN LEAVE THEIR HUSBANDS ONLY TO GO BACK TO THEM AWHILE LATER?

When a battered woman reconciles with her violent spouse, family and friends are often puzzled and frustrated. Sometimes her actions are misinterpreted as meaning that she really does need or like the abuse. In truth, however, the wife who leaves her husband faces a number of problems. As mentioned earlier, some women find it impossible to support themselves and their children. In addition, many violent men pressure their wives to come home. They may write daily letters, place numerous phone calls, make promises to reform, or even threaten to commit suicide. Some men tell their wives that they will find them and kill them unless they return. Finally, if a woman has never been on her own before, the whole experience can be very frightening. Often deprived of the emotional support of her family, she must not only find a way to provide for herself and children, but also cope with feelings of inadequacy, loneliness, fear and uncertainty. As time goes on, and intense memories of the abuse fade, she may ultimately decide that leaving her husband was a mistake. So, she goes back to give him "one more chance." Of course, sometimes a batterer does seek help and manages to overcome his problem. Unfortunately, however, this is still not the norm.

8. IF WE PROVIDE SHELTERS FOR BATTERED WOMEN, AREN'T WE JUST BREAKING UP FAMILIES? ISN'T THE DIVORCE RATE HIGH ENOUGH ALREADY?

The answer to this question depends on your definition of "family." In my opinion, a *real* family provides love and emotional support for all its members. Because of their care and concern for one another, they are stronger as a unit than as individuals. When there is violence in a home, it is absolutely impossible to create this kind of environment. Ideally, of course, counseling would eliminate the abuse, and the family could stay together. However, this is not always possible. To insist that the institution of "family" be preserved even though its members are being destroyed is unconscionable.

CHAPTER VIII

IF YOU ARE LIVING WITH VIOLENCE

If you are currently living with a violent man, you may at times feel that everything, including your life, is hopeless. There are no simple solutions and you should not expect to immediately solve all your problems or make all the right decisions. It will take time. Until you get out of the situation and/or until your husband gets help, here are some things for you to remember:

No one deserves to be beaten—
You do not have to earn the right not to be abused. Everyone is entitled to relationships which are satisfying and non-violent.

You are not to blame—
Regardless of what your husband or boyfriend may tell you, regardless of what friends or relatives may say, you are *not* responsible for the beatings. No one can *make* another person act brutally and violently. He may claim that you are the only person who can get him that angry, but you do not make him do anything he does not choose to do. Although counseling can help you both, you alone cannot make the marriage "work." You will not be able to stop the battering

100

simply by giving in to your mate's demands. You can never totally please him; he will always be able to find something wrong. Your husband will need professional help to learn to control his anger.

Talk to someone—

You need someone with whom you can discuss your problems and feelings, but be selective. Although friends and family members may be sympathetic, they probably cannot give you all the help you may need. I suggest you seek out a counselor. A counselor can be found through County Mental Health, the Department of Public Social Services, or by calling a hospital. However, under no circumstances should you continue with a counselor who: (1) tells you that you provoked your husband; (2) says that you can keep your husband from beating you by avoiding arguments, satisfying him in bed, etc.; (3) does not take your fears of physical harm seriously; or (4) tries to convince you that the abuse is not as bad as you think it is. These are clear indications that he or she does not completely understand the problem and you should seek help from another source.

A good counselor will also help you find ways of managing stress. You may have become accustomed to living with so much anxiety that you are not aware that you are constantly under a great deal of tension. Continued stress affects your emotional state and damages your body. Learning to relax may help you think more clearly and will reduce the possibility of your developing physical problems such as ulcers or high blood pressure.

Nurture yourself—

If you possibly can, try to do something special for yourself each day. This may take no more than five minutes and can be as simple as sitting quietly, reading a book, or going for a walk. Regardless of what you choose, it should be something for *you*, and no one else. Although you may find this difficult at first, let me assure you that focusing on your own needs is not selfish. You are important, too.

Get help for your children—

Even if you are not ready to seek counseling yourself, I urge you to get help for your children. You simply cannot provide them with all the support they need. Children who live with violence require professional help in dealing with their feelings and fears. I realize that you probably will not be able to discuss this with your husband. Your school may have a psychologist who could see your child during regular school hours.

CHAPTER IX

WHAT CAN BE DONE ABOUT WIFE ABUSE?

Community Involvement

It is very likely that major funding for future projects will have to come from the local community since Government is entering a period of austerity. Although not all areas will be able to provide comprehensive services, ideally a project would include these elements:

Public Education
Wifebeating has typically been a well-hidden crime and most people are still unaware of its scope and seriousness. In order to stimulate community involvement, a number of public education programs must be developed.

Churches and Service Organizations
Members of these groups need general information about domestic violence. In addition to providing speakers, it is important to make written material available. For example, House of Ruth produced a handbook which contained a section on legal and welfare rights, myths and facts about wife abuse, and emergency numbers. In one year's time, over 6,000 copies were distributed free of charge.

Helping Professions

Regardless of their training and background, most psychiatrists, psychologists, and counselors can benefit from workshops which teach methods of therapy for violent couples, and include a discussion of the dynamics, the social factors, and special problems associated with wife abuse. Furthermore, in order to offer comprehensive therapy, counselors must be aware of the social services (legal aid, educational opportunities, childcare facilities, etc.) available in their area.

School Programs

In terms of prevention, it is important to provide junior and senior high school students with information about domestic violence. Such material could be incorporated into a course o on Marriage and the Family. Girls need to be aware of the "warning signs" of a potential batterer, and both boys and girls could benefit from a discussion of sexual stereotypes.

Residential Facilities

There is still a pressing need for more safe houses. There is simply no other way to reliably protect women and children from further violence. Shelters also centralize services to their clients and allow women to discuss shared experiences and to give one another emotional suport.

Outreach

Hot-Line

A 24 hour hot-line is an important service which should provide crisis counseling, information, and referral to other agencies. It may be possible to avoid the cost of maintaining an office by having an answering service "patch" calls into the volunteers' homes.

Counseling

Ideally, counseling should be made available to women who remain with their husbands either by choice or by necessity. Group therapy has proven to be an effective and economical means of counseling victims of domestic violence. This setting encourages women to talk with one another, helping them to relieve feelings of isolation, embarrassment, and guilt. It is particularly valuable for a group to include a formerly battered woman who has been trained as a "peer counselor." Having "been there" herself, she had a special empathy and understanding and can also act as a positive role model.

Counseling for violent men must be provided as well. Many communities have no resources whatsoever for a batterer who wants to learn to control his anger. Recently, however, efforts have been made to develop methods of therapy. As with women, self-help groups may be the best approach.

Finally, it is vital that help be available to children from violent homes. These youngsters have special problems, and desperately need the attention of sensitive, caring adults. In some communities it may be feasible for school personnel (nurses, psychologists, etc.) to perform this function. It would also be advisable to train hotline volunteers to counsel children and adolescents, and then publicize the phone number in junior and senior high schools.

Changes in the Criminal Justice System

Police

The officer who responds to a "family disturbance" has a good chance of being wounded or killed. Better training for officers could not only reduce this risk, but could also improve the services provided. Some communities are experimenting with the idea of special "domestic violence teams," (an officer and a social worker) whose primary duty is to deal with "family disturbances."

Legal Aid

All communities should try to provide free legal counsel for women who have no financial resources. Low-cost services should also be available to those who cannot afford a private attorney but do not qualify for legal aid. There has recently been a trend toward training paralegals to help women fill out restraining orders, reserving the use of attorneys for more complicated and lengthy proceedings.

Victim Advocacy

Experience has shown that women who want to prosecute their husbands need special support services. In response to this need, programs have been developed in which a woman is given an advocate who helps her through the proceedings by attending all court appearances with her and providing information and emotional support throughout the trial.

Diversion Projects

Since it is unlikely that batterers will become rehabilitated while in prison, the courts must have some recourse besides jail or probation. For example, some communities have instituted diversion projects where a man can either choose to participate in counseling or face criminal prosecution. Since violent men are typically reluctant to enter therapy, the court mandate can, in some cases, provide the necessary incentive. However, if a man is not truly motivated to change, then such pressure may produce only external compliance. When the counseling period is over, the battering may well resume. Furthermore, unless wifebeating cases are prosecuted, both the criminal justice system and society in general will continue to consider wife abuse as a "family problem," not a crime. A possible solution to this problem would be to combine prosecution and diversion. In order to administer such a program, batterers would be classified as "tractable" or "intractable." A man would be considered "tractable" if he felt some guilt or remorse over his behavior, and had a genuine desire to learn to control his anger. This personal motivation would presumably make him a good candidate for a diversion program. By contrast, the "intractable" batterer may also be violent to others besides his spouse and usually sees nothing wrong with his behavior. When confronted by police or family members, he is likely to respond, "Why can't I beat her; she's my wife, isn't she?" Such a man would not be likely to benefit from counseling and could instead be prosecuted.

Steps in Establishing Community Programs

Unfortunately, there are still many communities which do not provide any services for battered women. If you would like to start a "grassroots" program in your area, there are certain steps you will need to take:

1. Locate interested individuals, clubs and agencies.
This can be done with a letter or by phone. You should contact, for example, the Department of Public Social Services, churches, police departments, YWCA and YMCA, probation department, local government officials, public and private counseling agencies, and service clubs (for both men and women). Once you have compiled a list, set a date for your first public meeting. Private citizens can be reached through newspaper articles. At the first meeting you will need to provide

information about domestic violence, discuss general plans for dealing with the problem, and try to identify those individuals who will have the time and personal commitment to form the "core" of your project. Don't be discouraged if only a few people sign up initially; it is better to have a small number of reliable, dedicated volunteers than to have a larger group that you might not always be able to count on. Hopefully, you will find individuals who will help with the next step.

2. Incorporation

If you plan to apply for grants you must form a non-profit, tax-exempt (state and federal) corporation; most funding agencies will only consider organizations that meet those requirements. You should consult a lawyer to help in this process. Unless you are willing to invest the money yourself, you will need to find an attorney who is willing to donate his or her services. Your attorney will also help you write bylaws and determine the structure of your organization.

3. Choosing a Board of Directors.

Generally speaking, you may have a board that is "working" or "advisory," or a combination of the two. Members of a "working board" are expected to be involved in the day-to-day activities of the organization. Sometimes they are even asked to make a specific time commitment. By contrast, advisory members are usually obliged only to attend board meetings. Until there is money to pay staff, you will need a board that is at least partially "working." In forming a board, you should also consider whether you will choose members for their money-raising ability, or for their expertise in law, social work, etc. The composition of your first board is particularly important; if you do not have an "umbrella agency," your directors are your only source of credibility. Eventually, of course, the quality of the service you provide will be a more important factor in the future success of your program. At that point you may want to consider some members on the board primarily because of their contacts for potential funding.

It is also necessary that at least one board member be a good public speaker. In the initial stages of your development, much of your time will be devoted to addressing a wide variety of agencies and service organizations. Since the demand for speakers can be high, you should have a minimum of two directors or other volunteers who can present your program to the public.

4.   Needs assessment.

This may be your most difficult task. As a rule, police records do not distinguish wifebeating from other domestic disturbance calls. If you have contacts in a police department or public service, you could ask them to conduct an informal poll. Check with all communities in outlying areas in order to locate any existing domestic violence programs; their figures will provide a basis for estimating the need in your area, and most shelter personnel are eager to help get new projects started. You should also compile a list of services (counseling, legal aid societies) that are currently available to the victims of domestic violence. This will help you avoid duplication in later program planning, and the information will also eventually be needed by your hotline volunteers.

5.   Program planning.

A comprehensive project to deal with domestic violence should provide protective shelter for women and children, counseling for all members of the family, legal aid, information on job training, employment, housing and child care, outreach (a hotline and drop-in counseling for women in the community), and a program of public education. You might want to consider forming a coalition of existing groups and agencies to meet your needs. Remember, you need not start out with a comprehensive project. For example, you may choose to first open a hotline. Your success with this program will establish your organization's credibility and will also provide much needed statistics.

6. Funding.

The specific means used to fund your project will, of course, depend upon the resources of your community. However, you will want to approach churches, service clubs, United Way, private foundations and city, county, and federal governments. You may also want to consider running your program under the auspices of an established agency such as the YWCA. The larger organization acts as an "umbrella" by lending its reputation and partial funding support to a new project. The "umbrella" also usually maintains a degree of control over the content and administration of your project. In short, you exchange autonomy for the opportunity to get started sooner.

If you intend to apply for grants, it is imperative that you find an experienced grant writer. Since proposal writing services are ordinarily rather expensive, you will need someone who is willing to donate the time. You may be able to find a student who is taking a course in "grantsmanship." Preparing a grant for your organization might fulfill a class requirement for him or her and provide you with "seed money."

Finally, it will be important for you to keep in contact with other organizations and agencies working in the field of domestic

110

violence. You might consider subscribing to RESPONSE, a publication of the Center for Women Policy Studies. This newsletter contains resource listings, funding alerts, book reviews, feature articles, and a calendar section. For more information, write to RESPONSE, Center for Women Policy Studies, 2000 P Street NW, Suite 508, Washington, DC 20036.

What You Can Do As An Individual

Of course, not everyone has the time to be involved in the development of community programs. However, there are certain things that each of us can do to help reduce the current level of domestic violence, and hopefully prevent future abuse.

Support existing programs—
A donation of five dollars or even a dollar will help. Your money will be put to good use, and small contributions really can make a difference. If you have some free time, you might also consider doing some volunteer work. Most shelters and domestic violence programs rely heavily on volunteers, and your involvement need not be major in order to be of value. Your commitment could be as extensive as being a hotline counselor or as intermittent as periodically helping address envelopes. Regardless, you will have the satisfaction of knowing that you have made a contribution toward the solution of a serious social problem.

Write a letter—
If you see advertising that portrays violence against women, *write a letter* or *call* the responsible party. For example, if the advertisement appeared in a magazine, you could voice your objections to

111

both the publisher and to the company who makes the product. Your telephone call or letter can make a difference; if enough individual complaints are received, someone will take notice. You should also consider writing to legislators and to state and local government officials. It must be made clear to our elected representatives that we are concerned about domestic violence and expect them to take an active role in providing funding for projects and in passing new laws.

Talk about the problem—

If there is something in this book that you found particularly interesting—or disturbing—talk about it. Wife abuse is a well-hidden crime which needs to be brought to public attention. Although you yourself may not be able to start a community program, your interest and concern could well inspire in others the energy and commitment necessary for the development of new services.

Raising Our Children

Assertiveness

As mentioned earlier, assertiveness does not mean being aggressive or "running roughshod" over everyone else. Rather, it is based on a strong sense of respect for oneself and for others. The child who is brought up to be assertive learns that he need not—and should not—use violence or other forms of intimidation in order to exercise his rights or satisfy his needs. For example, if an "assertive" man believes he has been taken advantage of, he can express those feelings at the time rather than "bottling up" his anger and resentment until they explode into violence. The "assertive" woman realizes that she has the right to demand a non-violent relationship and can do what is necessary to ensure that she is not abused.

Sex role models

Because sexual stereotypes are so pervasive in our society, parents must make a conscious effort if they want to avoid socializing their children into rigid, stereotyped sex roles. In my opinion, we should try to promote more flexibility in our definitions of "masculine" and "feminine" behavior. For example, it is not necessarily wrong for a woman to be dependent and submissive at times, just as it is not inherently bad for a man to be dominant or strong. However, it should also be socially acceptable for women to be assertive and independent, and men should be able to display the more tender, sensitive, and emotional side of their personalities. Ideally, a person would be allowed to develop his or her full potential, rather than be unduly restricted by social expectation. Perhaps if we could react to each other first as human beings, and second as male or female, we would begin to treat one another with more understanding and less violence.

FOOTNOTES AND REFERENCES

Chapter I — Myth and Reality

[1]Straus, M., Gelles, R., and Steinmetz, S. *Behind Closed Doors—Violence in the American Family*. New York: Anchor Press, 1980, p. 40.

Chapter II — Historical Precedents for Wifebeating

[1]O'Faolain, J., and Martines, L. (Eds.), *Not In God's Image*. New York: Harper & Row, 1973.

[2]Gies, F., and Gies, J. *Women in the Middle Ages*. New York: Thomas T. Crowell Company, 1978.

[3]Ibid.

[4]Ibid.

[5]Ibid., p. 38.

[6]Ibid., p. 39.

[7] Ibid.

[8] O'Faolain, *Not In God's Image*, p. 177.

[9] Gies, *Women in Middle Ages*.

[10] Coulton, G. *Medieval Panorama, the English Scene from Conquest to Reformation*. New York: Meridian Books, 1955.

[11] Gies, *Women in Middle Ages*, p. 46.

[12] Coulton, *Medieval Panorama*, p. 617.

[13] Gies, *Women in Middle Ages*.

[14] Ibid.

[15] Coulton, *Medieval Panorama*, p. 617.

[16] Gies, *Women in Middle Ages*.

[17] O'Faolain, *Not In God's Image*, p. 169.

[18] Coulton, *Medieval Panorama*.

[19] Camden, C. *The Elizabethan Woman*. Houston: Elsevier Press, 1952.

[20] Ibid., p. 148.

[21] Ibid.

[22] O'Faolain, *Not In God's Image*, p. 189.

[23] Ibid., p. 201.

[24] Camden, *Elizabethan Woman*.

[25] O'Faolain, *Not In God's Image*.

[26] Ibid.

[27] Camden, *Elizabethan Woman*, p. 116.

[28] Langley, R., and Levy, R. *Wifebeating — The Silent Crisis.* New York: Simon and Schuster, 1978.

[29] Camden, *Elizabethan Woman*.

[30] Ibid.

[31] Ibid.

[32] Hymowitz, C., and Weissman, M. *A History of Women in America.* New York: Bantam Books, 1978, pp. 22-23.

[33] Ibid.

[34] Ibid.

[35] Altbach, E. *Women in America.* Lexington: D.C. Heath and Company, 1974.

[36] Hymowitz, *History of Women in America*.

[37] Ibid.

[38] Ibid.

[39] Altbach, *Women in America.*

[40] Hymowitz, *History of Women in America*, p. 36.

[41] Ibid.

[42] Langley and Levy, *Silent Crisis*, p. 53.

[43] Ibid.

[44] Ibid., pp. 53-54.

[45] Hymowitz & Weissman, *History of Women in America.*

[46] Kraditor, A. (ed.), *Up from the Pedestal — Selected Writings in the History of American Feminism*. Chicago: Quadrangle Books, 1968, pp. 45-46.

[47] Ibid., p. 48.

[48] Ehrenreich, B., and English, D. *Complaints and Disorders — the Sexual Politics of Sickness*. Old Westbury: The Feminist Press, Glass Mountain Pamphlet No. 2., 1973, p. 28.

[49] Hymowitz & Weissman, *History of Women in America*, p. 75.

[50] Banner, L. *Women in Modern America — a Brief History*. New York: Harcourt Brace Jovanovich, Inc., 1974.

[51] Ibid.

[52] Ibid.

[53] Ibid.

[54] O'Neill, W. *Everyone Was Brave — The Rise and Fall of Feminism in America.* Chicago: Quadrangle Books, 1969, p. 332.

[55] Ibid.

[56] Freud, S. *Some Psychical Consequences of the Anatomical Distinction Between the Sexes.* In J. Strachey, (Ed. and trans.), The standard edition of *The Complete Psychological Works of Sigmund Freud, Vol. XIX.* London: The Hogarth Press, 1961, pp. 257-258.

[57] Lundberg, F., and Farnham, M. *Modern Woman — The Lost Sex.* New York: Harper & Brothers Publishers, 1947, p. 319.

[58] Friedan, B. *The Feminine Mystique.* New Dell Edition, New York: Dell Publishing Company, 1974, p. 13.

Chapter III — Social Factors Currently Contributing to the Incidence of Wife Abuse

[1] Stark, R., and McEvoy, J. "Middle Class Violence," *Psychology Today,* Nov. 1970, 52-54; 110-112.

[2] Borofsky, G., Stollak, G., and Messe, F. Sex Differences in Bystander Reactions to Physical Assault. *Journal of Experimental Social Psychology,* 1971, *7*, 313-318.

[3]London, J. Images of Violence Against Women. *Victimology*, 1977-78, Vol. 2, No. 3-4, 510-524.

[4]Larwood, L., and Wood, M. *Women in Management.* Lexington: D. C. Heath and Company, 1977.

[5]Brandwein, R., Brown, C., and Fox, E. Women and Children Last: The Social Situation of Divorced Mothers and Their Families. *Journal of Marriage and the Family*, August, 1974, *36*, 498-514.

[6]Payetter, G. How To Get and Hold a Woman. Cited in Stern, P. The Womanly Image: Character Assassination Through the Ages. In C. Adams & M. Briscoe (Eds.), *Up Against the Wall, Mother. . .On Women's Liberation.* Beverly Hills: Glencoe Press, 1971, p. 195.

[7]Morgan, M. *The Total Woman.* Paperback Edition, New York: Simon and Schuster, 1973, pp. 96-97.

[8]Andelin, H. *Fascinating Womanhood.* New Revised Edition, New York: Bantam Books, 1975, p. 261.

[9]Maccoby, E., and Jacklin, C. *The Psychology of Sex Differences.* Stanford University Press, 1974.

[10]Hartley, R. Sex-Role Pressures in the Socialization of the Male Child. In J. Pleck and J. Sawyer (Eds.), *Men and Masculinity.* Englewood Cliffs: Prentice-Hall, Inc. 1974, p. 12.

[11]Pleck, J., and Sawyer, J. (Eds.), *Men and Masculinity.* Englewood Cliffs: Prentice-Hall, Inc., 1974.

[12]Jouard, S. *The Transparent Self.* Princeton: Van Nostrand

Press, 1964.

[13]Ibid.

[14]Fasteau, M. Why Aren't We Talking? In J. Pleck and J. Sawyer (Eds.), *Men and Masculinity*. Englewood Cliffs: Prentice-Hall, Inc., 1974, p. 19.

[15]Symonds, A. Violence Against Women: The Myth of Masochism. *American Journal of Psychotherapy*, April, 1979, Vol. 33, 2, 161-173.

Chapter VI — Patterns of Interaction Among Violent Couples

[1]Walker, L. *The Battered Woman*. New York: Harper & Row, 1979.